JX
1252
.S35

D1035371

Lander College Library
Lander College
Greenwood, S. C. 29646

ECONOMIC WORLD ORDER?

THE MELLAND SCHILL LECTURES
*delivered at the University of Manchester
and published by the University Press*

ECONOMIC WORLD ORDER?

A BASIC PROBLEM
OF
INTERNATIONAL ECONOMIC LAW

by

GEORG SCHWARZENBERGER

OF GRAY'S INN, BARRISTER-AT-LAW
PROFESSOR OF INTERNATIONAL LAW IN THE UNIVERSITY OF LONDON
DIRECTOR, LONDON INSTITUTE OF WORLD AFFAIRS

105236

MANCHESTER UNIVERSITY PRESS
U.S.A.: OCEANA PUBLICATIONS INC.

Lander College Library
Lander College
Greenwood, S. C. 29646

© 1970 MANCHESTER UNIVERSITY PRESS

Published by the University of Manchester at
THE UNIVERSITY PRESS
316–324 Oxford Road, Manchester M13 9NR
UK ISBN: 0 7190 0448 9

U.S.A.
OCEANA PUBLICATIONS INC.
75 Main Street, Dobbs Ferry, N.Y. 10522
Library of Congress catalog card No. 70-132276
US ISBN: 0 379 11911 0

Distributed in India by
N. M. TRIPATHI (PRIVATE) LTD
Princess Street, Bombay 2

Printed in Great Britain by Butler & Tanner Ltd, Frome and London

CONTENTS

CONTENTS

vi

FOREWORD

By her will, the late Miss Olive Schill, of Prestbury, Cheshire, an old friend of the University, whose portrait is painted in Lady Katharine Chorley's *Manchester made them*, left the sum of £10,000 to the University in memory of her brother, Melland Schill, who died in the 1914–18 war. The annual income from this sum is to be used to promote and publish a series of public lectures of the highest possible standard dealing with international law.

Professor Georg Schwarzenberger is a world authority on international law and the author and editor of numerous articles, theses and textbooks on the subject. In particular, he has made the increasingly important field of international economic law very much his own. This subject is likely to grow daily more important, because politicians, parliamentarians and economists, in the last resort, rightly tend to seek the backing of fair and objective law for the projects of economic exchange and development on the success of which the material prosperity of the world depends. This work is therefore confidently commended to students and practitioners not only in the field of international law but also in the fields of international economics and international business.

Faculty of Law   B. A. WORTLEY
University of Manchester
January 1970

vii

LIST OF MULTILATERAL CONVENTIONS

Page

PREFACE

I should like to express my appreciation to the University of Manchester for its invitation to deliver the Melland Schill lectures.

Acceptance of this invitation forced me to formulate articulately two related thoughts which had been in my mind for some time. The first was that the exposition of the statics of international economic law which I had attempted elsewhere required to be supplemented by a more systematic exploration of the dynamics of international economic law. The second was that while on some levels of international economic relations the process of integration had rapidly accelerated, this was less true of other levels, and least of all of the world economy as a whole.

Thus the very limitation of this course to five lectures considerably helped in finding a workable approach to the treatment of these issues: to approach them from the periphery of global relations and reserve for future studies the analysis of the dynamics of international economic law on the various non-universal levels of international economic organisation. Hence the title of this series of lectures should be interpreted strictly and, as is more fully explained in the first and fifth lectures, the reader should not look here for a discussion of the trends in international economic law within any of the non-universal international economic institutions such as the General Agreement on Tariffs and Trade, the Organisation for Economic Co-operation and Development, the Council for Mutual Economic Aid, the European Free Trade Association or the European Communities.

Professor Wortley, as editor of the Schill lectures, and Professor Bin Cheng were kind enough to read the whole of the manuscript and made a number of helpful suggestions.

Dr Schwelb and Mr Kiernik of the Office of Legal Affairs of the United Nations greatly assisted by providing most of the material on which Dr E. D. Brown based the tables in Appendix 6. Dr Brown also read the proofs and prepared the index. In addition to Professor Cheng and Dr Brown, four other colleagues in the Faculty of Law of University College London

xi

and the London Institute of World Affairs, Miss Alpha Connelly, Mrs Margaret Homewood, Miss Eileen Landray and Mr Sutton, gave considerable help by checking references and providing other technical assistance in the preparation of the typescript.

University College London   G.S.
14 *January* 1970

Chapter I

FUNDAMENTALS

It is the purpose of this first lecture to explain the theme of the course, the methods applied and the terminology used.

I. THE THEME

The object of these lectures is to explore, in relation to international economic law, one of the basic jurisprudential problems, that is, the relation between law and order.

Empirically, it would be hard to disprove the generalisation that every legal system rests on a basis of power. This infra-structure may be unorganised or organised and it may be of a purely *de facto* character or have received legitimation of some kind. It is this order with its minimum of overriding commands and rules which is the foundation of all law.[1]

Like municipal law, international law has its underlying order. Such differences as, in this respect, exist between international law and the laws of mature communities result primarily from the differences in motivation predominant in societies and communities. Societies distinguish themselves from highly integrated communities by the prominence of individual or sectional interests, compared with those of the group as a whole. From this point of view, little difference exists between an unorganised international society of the pre-1914 type and the confederate international societies of the post-1919 and post-1945 periods.

The *de facto* systems of open power politics and power politics in disguise at the base of international societies both past and present are the orders conditioning international law.

In many of its aspects, international economic law is reasonably remote from the centre of world power politics, as compared with other branches of international law. Thus, for purposes of inter-disciplinary studies, it is worth exploring whether, and if so, how,

1

international economic law can perhaps dispense with, sublimate or otherwise modify its infra-structure of power.

In a world society, international law is, in the first place, global law and must be judged by its performance on this level. More highly integrated superstructures on regional or sectional levels are secondary manifestations of this world law. Yet their existence affects the overall picture as little as supranational institutions of a localised character alter the essentially confederate character of world society under the Charter of the United Nations. Similarly, if we inquire into the relation between law and order in international economic law, we are primarily concerned with this issue on a world scale. In supplementary studies, the impact of more limited orders, such as the consensual universalist orders of the Bretton Woods organisations and GATT or sectional groupings of the COMECON and Common Market type, must also be taken into account. Their existence may even permit forecasts on trends towards the further integration or disintegration on the decisive world scale. Yet first things must come first, and this course of five lectures will have to be limited to the primary problem: does an effective *world* order exist on which international economic law may securely rest?

These lectures also offer a welcome opportunity to make an inventory of the potentially relevant rules and to evaluate their significance from the point of view of an economic world order. This task has been made the more timely by the dogmatic if non-committal manner in which the International Law Commission and, following in its footsteps, the Second Vienna Conference of 1969 on the Law of Treaties have asserted the existence of peremptory rules of international law in the meaning of international *jus cogens*.[2] Thus it is left to doctrine to check in each branch of international law whether such rules actually exist and, if so, to determine their scope and contents.

II. METHODS

As in previous writings, the methods adopted in this book are those of an inductive, inter-disciplinary and relativist treatment of the subject.

It is *inductive* in that the applicable rules of international law are determined by reference to the hierarchy of law-creating processes, law-determining agencies and elements of such agencies laid down or implied in Article 38 of the Statute of the International Court of Justice, and legal principles are treated as mere abstractions, primarily for purposes of teaching and classification, from the operative rules of international law.

It is *inter-disciplinary* in that whenever the complexity of a phenomenon under investigation makes it advisable, free use is made of the assistance to be derived from other related disciplines of international studies, in particular that of international relations.

It is *relativist* in that any proposals *de lege ferenda* discussed are subjected to transcendental and immanent forms of criticism, characteristic of another related discipline: that of international legislation.

It has been suggested that international lawyers in general, and international economic lawyers in particular, should be forward looking, rather than backward looking, and be optimistic rather than pessimistic. It is understandable that such personal or professional advice regarding 'orientation' should be proffered. Yet it is hardly the task of the research student to adopt any attitude which is practically bound to lead to predestined results. It is his function to study the phenomenon under investigation without fear or favour. This may involve looking forward and backward. In any case, it means living in the present rather than in the past or future, however quickly this present may turn into a recent past. Whether, constitutionally or otherwise, a research student is an optimist or a pessimist is as little relevant as any other of his psychological characteristics. His preoccupation should be with reality and, if necessary, with the unmasking of pertinent ideologies and utopias, which divert, and may be intended to divert, attention from this concern.

Perhaps the term 'forward looking' should not be taken too literally and is meant to convey a present-day need for emphasis on the dynamic, rather than the static, aspects of law. Inevitably, concentration on the articulate formulation of the operative legal rules tends to create the impression of freezing the law as it stands at any particular moment. While the discharge of this task must always be the lawyer's concern, it need not preclude complementary experiments with trying to catch the law in motion and, perhaps,

3

even the law in the making. As always, it is a question of a proper balance, and on this opinions may differ.

In this respect, a point appears to have been reached in the study of international economic law when more attention may properly be paid to the dynamic aspects of the subject. Thus this series of lectures may also be viewed as the first of several attempts to complement the presentation of the statics of international economic law[3] by efforts to capture in a rationally verifiable form the ever-changing dialectic relation between freedom and order in world economic relations.

III. TERMINOLOGY

Some basic terms used in these lectures call for definition:

Community: a social group which is more highly integrated than a society (*q.v.*).

International economic law: the branch of international public law which is concerned with the ownership and exploitation of natural resources, production and distribution of goods, invisible international transactions of an economic or financial character, currency and finance, related services and the status and organisation of the entities engaged in such activities.

International economic order: primarily a basic but, essentially, a *de facto* system of international economic relations. The term *world economic order* emphasises the global character of such an international economic order.

In organised international society the terms 'international economic order' and 'economic world order' may also be employed in a second meaning: as synonyms of consensual international public orders or *jus cogens*. In this narrower sense, they are mandatory rules which may not be modified or abrogated by *inter se* agreements between individual parties.[4]

International economic quasi-order: an international *de facto* or *de jure* system which is too precarious to qualify as an international economic order. The systems of sanctions, including economic sanctions, under the Covenant of the League of Nations and Charter of the United Nations fall under this head.

International economic pseudo-order: ideologies or utopias which

4

serve to gloss over the absence of a *de facto* or *de jure* international economic order or the existence of a mere quasi-order. Doctrinal constructions of 'natural' rights of freedom of commerce or communication in unorganised international society offer classic illustrations of such pretensions. The legal character of these natural-law postulates is controversial. Thus, it is advisable to describe them as *normative* pseudo-orders. This term includes any rules which prescribe social standards of conduct and is wide enough to include moral and legal rules.

Jus cogens: law binding irrespective of the will of individual parties.

Jus dispositivum: law capable of being modified by contrary consensual engagements.

Legal public order: see under *Public order.*

Legal regime: a system of legal rules which are reasonably coherent but are too specialised or subordinate to qualify as a legal order.

Naturalist doctrine: writers who derive moral and legal principles from ethical postulates and other general propositions and regard these principles as morally and, frequently, also legally binding.

Partial international economic orders: international economic orders which, as a rule, are based on multilateral agreements or institutions but fall short of universality. If they aim at universality, they may be called *universalist.* While the United Nations Organisation has attained a state of near-universality, most of the relevant Specialised Agencies of the United Nations have not yet reached this point.

If the scope of such organs or institutions is regional in the geographical or common sense meaning of the term such as, for example, that of the European, Latin American, Asian and Far Eastern or African Economic Commissions of the United Nations, any economic order established on such a limited scale would be *regional.*

If such an order is of an exclusive or selective character, it is termed *sectional.* The Organisation for Economic Co-operation and Development and COMECON belong to this category, and so do, on the surface, regional organisations such as the Organisation of American States (*vide* Cuba) and the Organisation of African Unity (*vide* the Republic of South Africa).

In the case of specialised international institutions as, for instance, in the field of the international regulation of the production and marketing of primary products, an analogous distinction between *open* and *sectional* legal regimes is advisable. If, as in the case of the 1968 International Sugar Agreement, all the sectional interests involved are represented, the legal regime is an open system. If such regimes are limited to, for instance, producers, as in the case of the Organisation of Petroleum Exporting Countries, they are of a sectional character.

Like universal systems, partial systems do not necessarily constitute economic orders. They may be mere quasi-orders, pseudo-orders, regimes of a subordinate character or purely contractual arrangements of short-term duration.

Power: the mean between influence and force. Power distinguishes itself from *influence* by reliance on external pressure as a background threat, and from *force* by preference for achieving its ends without the actual use of physical pressure.

Power politics: a system of international relations in which groups consider themselves as ultimate ends; use, at least for vital purposes, the most effective means at their disposal, and are graded according to their weight in cases of actual or hypothetical conflict.

Power politics in disguise: the abuse of community (*q.v.*) concepts for purposes of power politics (*q.v.*).

Public order is the organisational framework of peace and other essential values protected by a society (*q.v.*) or community (*q.v.*). It includes, but is not limited to, basic legal rules which assist in the achievement of these objects and which, for this reason, have the character of *jus cogens* (*q.v.*). This facet of a public order may also be described as a *legal public order*.

Society: a loose type of association, as distinct from a community (*q.v.*).[5]

NOTES

[1] See, further, the paper on 'Law, order and legitimation in 23 *Current Legal Problems* (1970), p. 240 *et seq.*

[2] See, further, Carnegie Endowment for International Peace (European Centre), *The Concept of* Jus Cogens *in International Law* (1967), p. 117 *et seq.*, and Articles 53 and 64 of the 1969 Vienna Convention on the Law of Treaties, 8 *International Legal Materials* (1969), pp. 698 and 703.

6

[3] See, further, Hague Academy of International Law, *Recueil*, Vol. 117 (1966), p. 5 *et seq*.

[4] For a different use of the term 'international public order', as distinct from 'private order', in the conflict of laws—to describe national *jus cogens*—see, for instance, Article 3 of the Code of Private International Law (Bustamente Code), attached to the Habana Convention of 20 February 1928 (M. O. Hudson, *International Legislation*, Vol. IV, p. 2284).

[5] See, further, the 'Glossary of terms and maxims' in the present writer's *A Manual of International Law* (fifth edition, 1967), p. 625 *et seq*.

Chapter II

THE PROBLEM OF ECONOMIC WORLD ORDER IN UNORGANISED INTERNATIONAL SOCIETY

The contributions made to the problem of international economic order by the unorganised or, at the most, partly organised international society of the pre-1914 era lie primarily in the fields of *de facto* and pseudo-orders.

I. DE FACTO ORDERS

Perhaps the most powerful *de facto* order in pre-1914 days was that expressed in the words *Pax Britannica*. It rested on the combined might of the City of London and the Royal Navy. In the last resort, needy governments and private entrepreneurs had to take their cue from the City of London on what was expected from would-be 'host' countries of loans to be contracted. If the countries concerned were within reach of the British navy, applicants for credit also knew that the legal minimum standards with which the centre of liberal capitalism expected them to comply could, if required, be effectively enforced.

This international investor–debtor nexus and the policing function exercised by the British navy—occasionally, as in Venezuela (1902), reinforced by the navies of other creditor countries—and by the growing power of the United States in the western hemisphere formed the backbone of the international *de facto* order in pre-1914 economic relations. As is proved by the annual reports of the Council of Foreign Bondholders in London and the long list of defaulting foreign governments, local authorities and private enterprises, especially in Latin America and the Balkans, the system was operated with remarkable forbearance and an incredible willingness to throw good money after bad.

Some of the strain was taken off this international *de facto* order by two forms of direct domination: multi-national agglomerations such as the Ottoman, Austro-Hungarian and Russian empires and the colonial empires of the Western Powers. They made it possible for investors to deal with centralised governments in Constantinople, Vienna, Budapest and St Petersburg and, directly or indirectly, with Western colonial dependencies under laws adapted from the metropolitan legal systems of the colonial Powers concerned.

In the monetary field, the gold standard formed a complementary international *de facto* order. While it rested on parallel national legislation of the countries adhering to this standard, internationally it was purely of a *de facto* character.

By way of contrast, the gold and silver standards, with a fixed ratio of $1:15\frac{1}{2}$, as applied between the members of the Latin Monetary Union, constituted a consensual legal order. It was based on the agreement of 23 December 1865 between Belgium, France, Italy and Switzerland.[1] In law it extended only to those Continental and Latin American States which subsequently joined the Union but not to countries which unilaterally chose the gold franc as the basis of their national currencies.

II. PSEUDO-ORDERS

In so rudimentary a state of international economic order as existed in pre-1914 international society, it was not surprising that ideologies and utopias, advanced by interested parties and speculative minds in their own right, should fast outdistance reality.

1. Non-legal pseudo-orders

The economic theory of *laissez-faire* liberalism abounds with assumptions of automatically operating and self-adjusting systems of international economic order on the basis of rationally interpreted self-interest and general awareness of the common interest of all. This approach found its most renowned expression in the theories of a predestined harmony of economic interests and division of labour between industrialised and agricultural countries. It appeared to follow that freedom of trade corresponded closely to the common interest of mankind. Yet it did not take long for these ideals and ideologies to be exploded by the brutal question *cui bono?* and the interposition of the nation between the individual and mankind.

9

The champions of these liberalist theories considered them to be self-evident. It was implied in their propositions that compliance with these economic orders was purely voluntary. Thus these precepts might be ignored by those preferring un-reason to reason. In other words, the values put highest in liberalist economics could be overridden by economic systems based on different hierarchies of values. This was what happened before long in an age of growing nationalism and international insecurity.

2. *Normative pseudo-orders*

Two facets of naturalist doctrine are relevant for the discussion of the problem of economic international order: the assertion, irrespective of consent, of economic rights and freedoms of commerce and navigation and of immutable economic rights.

(*a*) *Economic rights and freedoms*. The naturalist doctrine of international law was prone to solve the problem of international economic order by deductive reasoning from first principles. In their conclusions, the pessimistic and optimistic variants of the natural-law schools of international law differ diametrically. While in the former the emphasis is on freedom, in the latter it is on order. In the former a society is assumed. In the latter a community (right at the other end of the sociological scale of pure types of social organisation) is taken for granted. Both schools do their best to refute each other. Yet they succeed merely in neutralising each other.

If naturalist philosophers happened to be conversant with the realities of international relations, they hedged by astute qualifications their propositions of alleged rights of freedom of commerce and navigation, supposed to exist irrespective of consent by the obligated party. For instance, these rights were described as being merely imperfect rights. To become perfect rights, they required the seal of consensual confirmation. In other words, save on a treaty basis, they did not exist or led a shadowy existence in the doctrine of natural and international law and were largely ignored in State practice.

Others arrived at similar conclusions by distinguishing between mankind, which was not viewed as an organised society, and nations which constituted such societies and were thought to have exclusive rights of property over their territories. Thus, admission

10

of foreigners to these territories could be made subject to permission and, if any government feared that such permission might endanger the well-being of its country, it remained free to refuse entry to any stranger. This was, for instance, the basis on which, in his *Institutes of Natural Law* (1756), a course of lectures delivered at St John's College, Cambridge, T. Rutherforth adjusted his theories to the political realities of his day.

(*b*) *International economic jus cogens.* In the form of, apparently, self-evident propositions of international *jus cogens*, it has been suggested that piracy *jure gentium* and slave-trading may not be legalised by agreement, and that any treaty to this effect is null and void.

It requires little effort to sort out truth from falsehood in these deceptive half-truths. We are not here concerned with the incompatibility of any such hypothetical treaty with one of the manifold consensual superstructures erected on the foundations of international customary law, nor with any subsequent reception of relevant multilateral treaties into international customary law, nor with any estoppel by recognition, limiting sovereign discretion to conclude treaties for the promotion of piracy or slave-trading. What we are concerned with is the position in classical international customary law. Only on this level is it possible to ascertain whether overriding legal rules exist which, at any particular time, may not be abrogated or modified by consent.

If States are parties to multilateral treaties outlawing piracy and slave-trading or are members of international institutions with objectives which are incompatible with these forms of 'free enterprise', the matter is settled not by reference to any 'higher' law, but by the rules of international customary law on the conflict of treaties. Similarly, if new States are recognised on the assumption that the prohibitions of piracy and slavery have become part of international customary law, it is not the character of these rules as *jus cogens* which estops States from making treaties to the contrary. It is the result of the interplay of the rules of international customary law on recognition and good faith.[2]

What is usually meant by the alleged character as *jus cogens* of the prohibitions of piracy and slave-trading is that such treaties cannot have any legal effect against third States and their subjects. This

11

conclusion is correct yet it rests on a different ground: the limitation to contracting parties of treaty effects, in particular regarding onerous obligations.

Any hypothetical treaty between States A and B legalising piracy and slave-trading would merely mean that contracting parties did not object to their own nationals becoming objects of piratical or slave-trading operations by the other contracting party or any of its nationals. Certainly the conclusion of such treaties would indicate a relapse of the parties into barbarism. It would not, however, prove that, under the international *customary* law of *unorganised* international society, treaties of this type would be void.

Actually, the whole history of the gradual outlawry by consent of slave-trading in the nineteenth century refutes assertions of an international *jus cogens* in this field on grounds other than consent in unorganised international society.[3]

III. THE REALITY

It must suffice to illustrate the reality of the situation in the international economic law of unorganised international society by three examples taken from State and judicial practice.

1. *The freedoms of international economic law.*

Long before the successive 'fathers' of international law began to speculate on rules of an international economic order, State practice faced the issue of the freedom of international communications.

In the eras of mercantilism and bullionism, governments treated freedoms of commerce and navigation—as, subsequently, these rights would be termed—as privileges to be granted to foreign merchants for adequate consideration. If foreigners were able to supply goods in short supply, especially armaments, or if they were likely to export local products which would bring bullion in return, they would be welcome. Otherwise, the enjoyment of freedom of commerce and navigation depended on the issue of individual or generalised safe conducts, the latter being subsequently incorporated into treaties of commerce and reformulated in terms of national or most-favoured-nation treatment in matters of commerce and navigation.

12

Such freedom of commerce as developed in Europe since the eleventh and twelfth centuries was hardly ever freedom of trade in the nineteenth-century meaning of the term. This was an extreme form of freedom of commerce, subject, even in the heyday of economic liberalism, to significant exceptions. Frequently, it was equality on a footing of foreign parity and, occasionally, equality on the basis of inland parity.

In the eyes of potential beneficiaries, equality of either type was merely the next best thing to preferential treatment in relation to other foreign merchants. Yet, from the point of view of the recipient, the best of all was the maximal form of freedom of commerce obtainable: a monopoly of trade. In cases in which European colonial expansion overseas stopped short of conquest, treaties granting trade monopolies or preferential treatment were the prizes most sought after by merchant adventurers and their militant trading companies.

Two conclusions emerge from the examination in historical perspective of the claims made by the naturalist doctrine of international law.

If anything appeared 'natural' to the representatives of the rising territorial State, it was the right of governments to grant on their own terms, or refuse, freedom of commerce and navigation.

More clearly than naturalist writers, and empirically rather than analytically, the clerks of princes realised the relativity and elasticity of principles such as freedom of commerce and navigation. It might mean equality of treatment on levels of national or most-favoured-nation treatment. Yet, if opportunity offered itself, these freedoms could also be employed to secure preferential treatment or even monopolies of trade.

In treating these principles as purely optional, the practice of international law made another major discovery. Actually, this preceded the articulate formulation of these principles in abstract form: the availability of optional standards such as those of ancient, customary, identical, preferential, most-favoured-nation and national treatment. Subsequently, these standards served to define in concrete and verifiable terms the form in which these freedoms were to be secured.

In other words, the practice of States ignored any pretensions to

13

the enjoyment of economic freedoms, short of consensual commitments or gradually evolving rules of international customary law in this field. Actually, the only relevant standard which became incorporated in international customary law—that is, the minimum standard of international law regarding the treatment of the persons and property of foreign nationals—was but the product of innumerable treaty clauses which, in the pre-1914 period, came to be taken for granted as legally binding between civilised nations.

2. *The St Lawrence controversy*

In a classic exchange of arguments between the United States and British governments in 1824 on freedom of navigation on the river St Lawrence, the United States government claimed freedom of communications with the Atlantic ocean through the river St Lawrence for the inhabitants of the United States 'upon the same ground of natural right and obvious necessity heretofore asserted by the Government on behalf of the people of other portions of the United States, in relation to the River Mississippi'.[4] Correspondingly, the United States government treated evidence to the contrary from European State practice as an abuse rather than an exercise, of territorial sovereignty. On the doctrinal level, the United States government relied on the authority of a whole string of naturalist writers from Grotius to Vattel.

As might be expected, the British government emphasised in its reply the qualifications of the 'natural' rights which the more discerning among naturalist writers had made. It then played its trump card: a request for acknowledgment by the United States of a reciprocal 'natural' right of British subjects for freedom of navigation on the river Mississippi.

The dispute was settled by the Reciprocity Treaty of 5 June 1854 between the two countries. In return for the grant of tariff reciprocity, and subject to a right of revocation upon notice, the British government granted freedom of navigation on the river St Lawrence and its canals to the inhabitants of the United States on the basis of the standard of national treatment.[5] Today this freedom of navigation rests on Article 26 of the Treaty of Washington of 8 May 1871, that is, on a purely consensual basis.[6]

14

3. The Anzilotti–Huber joint opinion

Perhaps the clearest refutation of any claim of rights of communications to be of an absolute character is to be found in the powerful joint dissenting opinion in the *Wimbledon* case (1923), handed down by the two outstanding members of the Permanent Court of International Justice, Anzilotti and Huber.

In this case, all the parties to the dispute accepted the treaty character of the right of innocent passage of foreign ships through the Kiel canal. Even so, Judges Anzilotti and Huber held that, in the case of any such predominantly economic treaty rights, a presumption in favour of the territorial sovereign must be implied. The littoral State could not be expected to have limited its sovereignty in relation to situations in which its economic duties might clash with overriding duties of a political character. In the case before the Court, these were Germany's duties as a neutral power in the war between Poland and the Soviet Union.[7]

One final reflection may be helpful. If freedom of commerce and navigation were 'natural' rights, so would be the right of sovereignty. Thus, again, propositions based on natural law as such prove to be self-neutralising and self-defeating. Since any of these rights rests on one of the two law-creating processes recognised in unorganised international society—international customary law and treaty law—the question of the precedence of any right under international customary law (as is that of national sovereignty) over rights of treaty law (as are the freedoms of commerce and navigation in artificial maritime waterways) is purely a matter of treaty interpretation.

NOTES

[1] 20 Martens (1st ser.), p. 688. See also 21 *ibid.* (2nd ser.), p. 65, and 2 *ibid.* (3rd ser.), p. 918.

[2] See, further, Hague Academy of International Law, *Recueil*, Vol. 87 (1955), p. 228 *et seq.*

[3] See, for instance, *Le Louis* (1817), 2 Dodson 210; *United States* v. *La Jeune Eugénie* (1822), 2 Mason 409; *The Antelope* (1825), 10 Wheat. 66; *Buron* v. *Denman* (1848), 2 Exch. 167; H. Wheaton, *Enquiry into the Validity of the British Claim to a Right of Visitation and Search of American Vessels Suspected to be Engaged in the African Slave-trade* (1842), pp. 16 and 68 *et seq.*; Oppenheim's *International Law*, Vol. I (first edition, 1905), p. 347, note 1, and *ibid.*, Vol. I

(eighth edition, 1955, ed. H. Lauterpacht), p. 733. See also below, Chapters III and IV.

[4] H. A. Smith, *Great Britain and the Law of Nations*, Vol. I (1935), p. 334.

[5] Article 4 (44 *Br. and For. St. Papers*, p. 25, at p. 28).

[6] Article 26 (61 *ibid.*, p. 51).

[7] Publications of the Court, Series A, No. 1, p. 15, at p. 36.

Chapter III

THE PROBLEM OF ECONOMIC WORLD ORDER IN THE LEAGUE OF NATIONS ERA

In spite of the failure of the League of Nations, this experiment still has instructive lessons to teach. In particular, this applies to a world which, in the United Nations, is based on the same confederate principle.

I. THE DE FACTO ECONOMIC ORDER OF THE POST-1919 ERA

The gold standard, as operated before 1914, was subjected to increasing interference from the first world war onwards and, on being abandoned by the United Kingdom, the United States of America and other countries by 1933, broke down completely. In defiance of all liberalist advice poured out by a powerless League Secretariat, individual experts and world economic conferences, the post-1919 world settled down to practices of growing protectionism and autarchism.

In retrospect, two of these developments appear more significant than the shower of reports and resolutions which had emanated from Geneva.

One was the development of the Soviet Union into a major autarchist bloc, based on rigorously applied import and export monopolies. Thus the foundations were laid for a sectional economic order in the post-1945 world to come.

The other was the abandonment by the United Kingdom and the members of the British Commonwealth of the tenet that the natural riches of the British colonial empire were at the disposal of the world at large on equal terms for all. In the Ottawa agreements of 1932 a further sectional order, based on the standard of preferential treatment, was created.[1]

17

Perhaps even more significant than any other feature of the *de facto* economic 'order' of the post-1919 era was a practice which had grown up in the years of the Great Depression. Producers of primary products such as maize, wheat and coffee took a hand in solving the problem of 'overproduction'. In utter despair, they burned their crops, and governments tried to assist this 'policy' further by paying subsidies to farmers for restricting their areas of cultivation. Yet the feeding back of butter to cows in the European Economic Community—as an alternative to shovelling it into the North Sea—serves as a warning that, from the consumer's point of view, the difference between the *de facto* order of a liberalist economy and a partly planned supranational order may be but marginal.

II. THE DE JURE ECONOMIC ORDER
OF THE POST-1919 ERA

Three aspects of the legal order or quasi-order—a question better left open at this stage—of the period between the first and second world wars call for consideration: the significance of Article 23 of the League Covenant; the attempts made during this era to create potential international economic *jus cogens* through multilateral treaties, and the fate of Article 16 of the League Covenant, in particular the experiment made in the Italo-Ethiopian war with the application of economic sanctions.

1. *Article 23 of the League Covenant*

In this article a number of rules are set out which might have become the nucleus of a substantial international economic order on a universalist treaty basis: the establishment and maintenance of fair and humane conditions of labour; just treatment of colonial subjects; supervision by the League of Nations of the execution of agreements relating to traffic in women and children and in dangerous drugs, the armaments trade with countries in which control of this traffic was considered necessary 'in the common interest' and, finally, the establishment and maintenance of freedom of communications and equitable treatment for the commerce of all member States.

18

The only trouble with this catalogue was that all endeavours towards these ends were 'subject to and in accordance with the provisions of international conventions existing or hereafter to be agreed upon' by the members of the League of Nations.

In the advisory opinion on *Railway Traffic between Lithuania and Poland* (1931), the Permanent Court of International Justice examined the character of the obligations entered under Article 23(*h*) of the Covenant. These obligations—and the same applied to those undertaken under all the other paragraphs of this Article—were mere *pacta de contrahendo*.[2]

2. *Consensual jus cogens*

Six attempts to create potential international *jus cogens* in the economic field under the auspices of the League of Nations call for attention: conventions on slavery, traffic in women and children for immoral purposes, the circulation of obscene publications, the illicit manufacture and traffic in dangerous drugs, the suppression of counterfeiting currency, and control of the arms trade.

(*a*) *Slavery*. The parties to the Slavery Convention of 25 September 1926[3] undertook, so far as they had not already taken the necessary steps, to prevent and suppress the slave trade and bring about 'progressively and as soon as possible' the complete abolition of slavery in all its forms.

The contracting parties realised the danger that compulsory or forced labour could develop into conditions analogous to slavery. Yet, in trying to limit forced labour, they found themselves compelled to recognise the legality of compulsory or forced labour for public purposes. Where it continued to be employed for other than public purposes, they undertook to 'endeavour progressively and as soon as possible to put an end to the practice'.

The contracting parties also reserved the right to exempt from the application of the Convention 'some or all' of the territories under their sovereignty, jurisdiction, protection, suzerainty or tutelage in respect of 'all or any provisions' of the Convention. Moreover, each of the parties was to be free to denounce the Convention, with effect one year after notification to the Secretary-General of the League of Nations.

In line with the evolution of the international prohibition of

19

slavery since the Vienna Declaration of 1815 against the Slave Trade,[4] this Convention offers evidence for four propositions:

(i) The parties considered slave-trading and slavery incompatible with the 'general principles which should guide their commercial and civilising action'.

(ii) They realised that slave-trading and slavery, as practised in the nineteenth century, had become localised issues, largely limited to the Islamic parts of Africa and the Near East.

(iii) They were even more conscious of the fact that, on a potentially unlimited scale, a new menace had arisen: forced labour as the twentieth-century equivalent of slavery. They—and, subsequently, the International Labour Organisation—decided to deal gingerly with this more relevant issue.

(iv) Compared with the elaborate effort made in the General Act for the Repression of the African Slave Trade (2 July 1890),[5] the 1926 Convention proved that the price of a more generalised application of treaty law was—and is—likely to be a reduced degree of stringency and a greater measure of concessions to the susceptibilities of national sovereignty.

Thus any suggestion that the Slavery Convention of 1926 was different in kind from the earlier efforts to deal with this scourge through bilateral and multilateral treaties would be hard to substantiate.

(b) *Traffic in women and children for immoral purposes.* The matter is codified in the Convention of 30 September 1921 on the Suppression of the Traffic in Women and Children[6] and the further Convention of 11 October 1933 on the Traffic in Women of Full Age.[7]

The League of Nations took up the work where it had been left in the conventions of 1904 and 1910 on the subject.[8] It did its best to universalise rules, originally intended for the protection of European women (*traite des blanches*).

Both conventions contain provisions, permitting reservations and contracting-out clauses similar to those of the Slavery Convention of 1926.

(c) *Traffic in obscene publications.* Simultaneously with the 1910 Conference on Traffic in Women, another international conference in Paris adopted a Draft Convention on the Suppression of the Circulation of, and Traffic in, Obscene Publications.[9] It failed, however, to come into operation.

A conference convened under the auspices of the League of Nations resulted in a new Convention of 12 September 1923 on the Suppression of the Traffic in Obscene Publications.[10] Like the conventions previously discussed, this Convention creates internationally prescribed municipal criminal law and contains corresponding escape and denunciation clauses.

In 1928, the Council of the League of Nations considered the advisability of calling a further conference on the subject, but decided that the time was not yet ripe for such an additional effort.

(d) *Illicit manufacture and traffic in dangerous drugs.* Starting with the Opium Convention of 23 January 1912, in force since 1920,[11] a series of conventions on the control of the manufacture and trade in opium and other dangerous drugs culminated in the Convention of 26 June 1936 for the Suppression of the Illicit Traffic in Dangerous Drugs.[12]

These conventions are based on the same patterns as those discussed above: prohibitions and restrictions, backed by the creation of criminal offences under the municipal laws of the contracting parties; extension of criminal jurisdiction; inclusion of the criminal offences created among extraditable crimes, and co-operation between national central offices for the furtherance of the objectives aimed at in these conventions.

Again, these conventions are subject to denunciation, at the most after five years and with effect one year after denunciation.

(e) *Suppression of Counterfeiting currency.* In a tradition which can be traced back to the Treaty of 5 November 1878 between the members of the Latin Monetary Union,[13] the League of Nations took the initiative in establishing in 1926 a mixed committee on counterfeiting currency. Its deliberations led to an international conference held in 1929 and a Convention on the Suppression of Counterfeiting Currency, opened for signature on 20 April 1929 and in force since 22 February 1931.[14]

The chief objects of the Convention were to achieve a measure of unification of the criminal laws of the parties to the Convention; an extension of national jurisdiction to prosecute offences covered by the Convention; the inclusion of such crimes among extraditable offences in extradition treaties concluded and to be concluded between contracting parties, and close co-operation between national central offices, to be organised in the countries of each of the contracting parties.

According to Article 5 of the Convention, no distinction may be made regarding the punishment of criminal offences relating to domestic and foreign currencies. This provision is especially safeguarded by a prohibition to subject it 'to any condition of reciprocity by law or by treaty'.

The article has a threefold legal meaning:

(i) It assures to the contracting parties the application of a standard of equality of treatment (national standard) regarding the punishment of offences against foreign currencies and thus avoids any invidious discrimination in this respect.

(ii) Within the limits of Article 22 of the Convention, contracting parties may add reservations to their acts of ratification or accession. Yet, if they were permitted to make reservations regarding the prohibitions contained in Article 5, this would enable them to contract out of obligations which the contracting parties treated as essential. Thus, individual contracting parties may not modify the rule laid down in Article 5 by way of reservations or *inter se* agreements.

(iii) In relation to third parties, the prohibitory rules of Article 5 cannot apply. It would, however, be in the spirit of the Convention to interpret Article 5 of the Convention so as to preclude any party to the Convention from entering into an agreement with any third party that would conflict with Article 5.

Thus, in aiming at the prevention of agreements between individual parties which are incompatible with the main objectives of the Convention and at restraining contracting parties from concluding such agreements with third parties, Article 5 fulfils the typical functions of consensual international *jus cogens*.

Like the other conventions discussed above, the Convention may be denounced, with effect from one year after denunciation.

(*f*) *Control of the arms trade.* In paragraph 5 of Article 8 of the League Covenant, the members of the League of Nations agreed that the manufacture by private enterprise of munitions and implements of war was 'open to grave objections'. The League Council was to advise how the 'evil effects attendant upon such manufacture' were to be prevented, due regard being had to the necessities of those members of the League who were not able to manufacture the munitions and implements of war necessary for their safety.

In the eyes of public opinion, the private arms trade had been one of the major factors contributing to the first world war. Woodrow Wilson and Lord Robert Cecil shared this view and, during the drafting of the Covenant, introduced a more strongly worded clause on the subject. In this draft clause agreement between the contracting parties was expressed that munitions and implements of war 'should not be manufactured by private enterprise', and the League Council was 'directed' to advise 'how this practice can be dispensed with'.[15]

In a memorandum submitted to Lord Cecil, the British Admiralty voiced objections to the contemplated suppression of the private manufacture of arms. In particular, it emphasised the advantages of any such prohibition to aggressive Powers and the dangers it presented to States lacking armament industries of their own.[16] This latter objection was also voiced by Portugal and, as an amendment to the previous draft article, found its way into the final text of Article 8.[17]

This drafting history explains the indecisiveness of the text of paragraph 5 of Article 8 of the League Covenant as finally adopted.[18]

Subject to the same reservations as in relation to all other duties which the League of Nations was to perform under Article 23 of the Covenant, the League was also entrusted with the general supervision of the trade in arms and ammunition with the countries in which the control of this traffic was thought to be necessary 'in the common interest'.

As in other fields, so in that of arms control, the members of the League of Nations tried their hand at 'updating' the work done by an earlier generation: the Brussels General Act of 2 July 1890.[19] This Act and the supplementary Brussels Protocol of 22 July 1908[20] had been primarily concerned with the repression of the African slave trade. In this context, however, it proved essential also to cope with the export and transport of arms to the areas infested by slave traders and inhabited by tribes willing to employ such arms in internecine wars for the supply of 'black ivory'. Thus provision was made for the control of the importation, sale and transportation of firearms and ammunition in defined portions of Africa and the Near East.

The first of the post-1919 efforts was the St Germain-en-Laye Convention of 10 September 1919 on the Control of Trade in Arms and Ammunition.[21] In its preamble, the draftsmen had referred to the 'danger to peace and public order', which resulted from the accumulation of arms and ammunition left over from the first world war.

Subject to the grant of licences, the export of specified arms and ammunition was prohibited. Similarly, import of arms and ammunition into extensive areas in Africa and the Near East and their transportation in maritime zones surrounding these areas, in particular in small native vessels, was restricted. The Convention entered in force on 20 March 1921. Yet many of the arms-producing States failed to ratify it.

In 1925 a new attempt was made, and a further Convention on the Suppression of the International Trade in Arms and Ammunition and in Implements of War was opened for signature on 17 June 1925.[22] It contained an even more impressive list than the 1919 convention of armaments which were to be subject to the regime under the Convention. Although it was less stringent than the 1919 convention, it failed to obtain the minimum of fourteen unconditional ratifications required to bring it into operation.

As had been clear in 1919 and became more evident in the deliberations preceding the World Disarmament Conference of 1932, the problem was more complex than the prohibition or control of the private trade in arms. Any limitation on these lines affected arms-producing countries less than non-producing countries, and least of all those arms-producing countries whose arms production was in public hands. Thus effective international control of the trade in arms depended on effective international control of the manufacture of arms, and to ask for this was to cry for celestial bodies far beyond the moon.[23] In an atmosphere rapidly changing into one of

24

a pre-war era, another prolonged attempt at the creation of economic *jus cogens* had come to nought.

(*g*) *Evaluation.* In order to assess the contribution made by these conventions to the establishment of a legal order in international economic relations, two related questions require answers. The first is whether, and if so in which sense, these conventions constitute international criminal law, and the second is whether these conventions have created rules of international *jus cogens*.

The term 'international criminal law' is employed in at least six different senses.[24] These conventions offer illustrations of internationally prescribed municipal criminal law. Yet, if only at the risk of misunderstandings, it is possible to term such municipal law 'international criminal law'. Actually, two of the conventions discussed contain express reservations on this very point. Participation in, for instance, the Traffic in Dangerous Drugs Convention of 1936 is not to be interpreted as affecting any party's 'attitude on the general question of criminal jurisdiction as a question of international law'.

Little doubt exists that prohibitory rules have been created by these conventions. Yet, unless the term *jus cogens* is inflated so as to include any consensual rules of a prohibitory character which are not mere sham rules (as, for instance, 'so far as possible' clauses), the fact that a rule is prohibitory, by itself, hardly justifies its description as international *jus cogens*.

To achieve this distinction, it must be sufficiently important to form part of a reasonably stable international legal order. Some evidence for this may be thought to be furnished by the number of parties to conventions embodying such rules and the length of the commitment in terms of time. These are contributory factors in assessing the character of a rule as one of consensual *jus cogens*. Yet another aspect of the matter is more decisive. It is whether individual parties to such a multilateral treaty are allowed to make subsequent *inter se* arrangements, modifying or abrogating their multilateral obligations.

The conventions discussed have been selected for the very reason that, in subject-matter, they are sufficiently important to contain rules which qualify potentially as rules of international economic *jus cogens*. Yet three doubts appear to counsel caution:

25

(i) The parties to these conventions remain free to apply these rules to parts of their territories only.

(ii) The parties may qualify their ratifications and accessions by far-reaching reservations. Admittedly, these reservations must be acceptable to the other contracting parties. Yet, if they are not acceptable to some, the contracting party which has made reservations remains a party in relation to those who do not object to these reservations.

(iii) Parties may denounce these conventions immediately or, in some cases, after the lapse of, at most, five years, and with short-term effect.

Any such denunciation leaves unaffected the duties of States under international customary law. Thus it remains to be explored whether any of the consensual rules discussed may be considered to be declaratory of international customary law as it stood at the time when the convention discussed was concluded, or as it has since developed. Moreover, in any such case, it would have to be further examined whether the rule of international customary law in question was one of *jus cogens* and, therefore, unalterable on a consensual basis.

In performing this task, it is advisable to guard against an understandable error. Some of the objectives of these conventions form an essential part of the standard of civilisation, especially as this is understood in Western countries. Yet is the standard universally or generally accepted on a global scale? If this be so, has this standard been incorporated in international customary law, and not only as an ordinary rule of this body of law, but as part of *jus cogens*?

The question whether the objectives of all but one of these conventions are postulated by the standard of civilisation can probably be answered in the affirmative. A doubt arises regarding the counterfeiting of enemy currency in time of war. Yet it can probably be resolved on other grounds which make it irrelevant whether, according to the standard of civilisation, even enemy States benefit from this rule.

For two reasons, counterfeiting enemy currency may be thought to be unlawful.

The first objection is that the circulation of forged enemy currency cannot be limited to enemy territory and, in the typical case, appears to affect neutral States and their nationals more adversely than the enemy. Exceptional cases of agents parachuted into enemy territory apart, the normal situation is the one illustrated by 'Operation Cicero' in the second world war: the bringing into circulation of forged enemy banknotes in neutral countries.

The second objection relates to the law of belligerent occupation. If the forged currency were enemy currency in circulation in occupied territory, its issue in large quantities would constitute a threat to the economy of the occupied territory concerned and an easy way of evading the duty of the occupying Power to respect private property and discharge its own obligations as an administering authority.

To constitute a breach of the laws of war and neutrality, the forgery of enemy currency must be attributable to the belligerent State. Thus, this argument is not conclusive regarding the illegality under international customary law in time of peace of the forgery of the currency of a foreign State by private individuals.

Whether, in any or all of these cases, the obligations of the standard of civilisation have become incorporated into international customary law or may at least be regarded as general principles of law recognised by civilised nations is a question of evidence. Yet it is important to be clear about the evidence for which we are looking.

In all the conventions discussed, prohibitory rules, backed by criminal sanctions under municipal law, have been created. Thus the relevant rules of international customary law or general principles of law recognised by civilised nations would consist of prohibitions of slavery, traffic in women and children for immoral purposes, the circulation of obscene publications, the counterfeiting of currency and the illicit manufacture of, and traffic in, dangerous drugs.

As with many other rules of international customary law, so the rules prohibiting slavery and slave-trading are probably *by now* rules of general international customary law. It is a matter of opinion whether this is because most of the sovereign and equal members of the United Nations have reached so high a standard of civilisation that, in their view, these profitable institutions and enterprises have become unacceptable and illegal. What is certain is that, in all but the more remote—but oil-producing—parts of the Islamic world, domestic slavery of the traditional type appears to have outlived

27

its social and economic usefulness. Thus, retrospectively it is easy to moralise on the subject or even to elevate these prohibitions into rules so basic as, irrespective of their embodiment in multilateral treaties, to qualify them as rules of international *jus cogens*.

Yet, when it comes to the prohibition of forced labour, the number of States who are willing to treat this prohibition—even with reservations regarding compulsory public service or penal servitude —as a rule of international customary law or a general principle of law recognised by civilised nations is likely to diminish sharply.[25]

Similarly, strong moral cases can be made for the prohibition of the traffic in women and children for immoral purposes, the circulation of obscene publications, and the illegal manufacture of, and traffic in, dangerous drugs. Evidence for the translation of these moral judgments into rules of international law other than on the basis of consensual engagements appears, however, to be lacking.[26]

As might be expected in an international economy, still largely relying on the free or controlled exchange of foreign currencies, some evidence can be found for the proposition that, by international customary law, the counterfeiting of foreign currencies is prohibited.[27] Leaving aside in this context the more specialised rules on the subject in the laws of war and neutrality, this means that, under this rule of international customary law, every subject of international law is bound to make adequate provision for the punishment of such offences in its own criminal law.

Two cases provide considerable evidence in this direction: *Emperor of Austria* v. *Day and Kossuth* (1861), decided by the English Court of Chancery and the Court of Appeal in Chancery, and *United States* v. *Arjona* (1887), decided by the United States Supreme Court.

The essential facts in *Emperor of Austria* v. *Day and Kossuth* were that Kossuth, while resident in England as a political refugee, had given an order to Messrs Day and Sons to print a large quantity of Hungarian paper currency, to be issued after the overthrow of the then prevailing Hungarian regime. The notes printed by Messrs Day and Sons were distinct from those actually in circulation in Hungary, but could be mistaken by the ordinary public for Hungarian banknotes and, in this sense, could be described as spurious.

The British government refused the request made by the Austro-

28

Hungarian ambassador to interfere directly in the affair. It was left to the Austrian Emperor as King of Hungary to sue in Chancery, and the defendants were ordered to deliver up the Hungarian notes printed, for purposes of cancellation, and were restrained from printing any further such notes.[28]

The case was fully argued in the Court of Chancery and the Court of Appeal in Chancery. Vice-Chancellor Stuart held that the printing of these notes for issue in the contemplated exercise of a power hostile to that of the plaintiff, who was the head of a friendly State, was contrary to English and international law:

The regulation of the coin and currency of every State is a great prerogative right of the sovereign power. It is not a mere municipal right or a mere question of municipal law. Money is the medium of commerce between all civilised nations; therefore, the prerogative of each sovereign State as to money is but a great public right recognised and protected by the law of nations. A public right, recognised by the law of nations, is a legal right; because the law of nations is part of the common law of England.[29]

The Vice-Chancellor added that unless 'this universal law' were adopted in its full extent by the common law, England 'must cease to be part of the civilised world.'[30] Referring to legislation passed in 1830 to the effect that the forgery or counterfeiting of the paper money of any foreign sovereign or State was a felony, he further held:

This statute is a legislative recognition of the general right of the sovereign authority in foreign States to the assistance of the laws of this country, to protect their rights as to the regulation of their paper money as well as their coin, and to punish, by the law of England, offences against that power. The friendly relations between civilised countries require, for their safety, the protection by municipal law of an existing sovereign right of this kind recognised by the law of nations.[31]

In the Court of Appeal in Chancery, Lord Campbell, L.C., emphasised that, while there was no ground for imputing any fraud to Kossuth, he had asserted in the printed notes that they were guaranteed by the Hungarian State, and that he had authority to sign them in the name of the Hungarian nation. What was decisive was that, 'unauthorised by the English government', the defendants, both of whom were subject to the court's jurisdiction, had interfered with the proprietary rights of the head of a friendly State.[32]

In the concurring judgments handed down by Knight Bruce, L.J.,

29

and Turner, L.J., it was made even clearer that the rights of the plaintiff and his subjects, whom a sovereign was entitled to represent, were of a civil, and not a public or criminal, character, and the acts complained of constituted injuries to property, actual or prospective.[33] Thus, with minor emendations, the Vice-Chancellor's decree was ordered to stand, and the defendants' appeal was dismissed.

In *United States* v. *Arjona*[34] a United States statute of 16 May 1884[35] was under attack on constitutional grounds. Under the Statute, the counterfeiting of foreign notes, banknotes and other securities of foreign governments was made punishable.

The United States Supreme Court held that, under the constitution of the United States,[36] Congress was expressly authorised to define and punish offences against the law of nations, and that the law of nations required every government to use 'due diligence' to prevent the commission in its territory of wrongs to another nation with which it was at peace.

More particularly, the Supreme Court relied on the *dictum* in Vattel's *Le Droit des gens* (1758) that 'if one nation counterfeits the money of another, or if it permits counterfeiters to do so and protects them, it does a wrong to that nation'.[37]

Both cases go a long way towards establishing a rule of international customary law, postulating the punishment under municipal law of the counterfeiting of foreign currencies. Yet in *Emperor of Austria* v. *Day and Kossuth* all that was actually at issue was the right to institute civil proceedings in England for the purposes of restraining the issue of spurious foreign banknotes. Similarly, in *United States* v. *Arjona*, the emphasis was on the *right* of the federal government under the United States constitution to pass criminal legislation regarding the counterfeiting of foreign banknotes rather than on its duty by international law to pass such legislation.

Even so, taken together with other relevant material from diplomatic practice, the available evidence in favour of a rule of international customary law, requiring the punishment under municipal law of the forgery of foreign currency, is stronger than the evidence that can be adduced on a good many other rules of international customary law. On this footing of relativity, the rule may be considered to exist. It is, however, limited to currencies issued by *recognised* States and governments. If the argument advanced above

30

on the prohibition of the forgery of enemy currency is not accepted,[38] the rule is further qualified by the condition that the States involved are in a state of peace with each other.

As with other prohibitions of a similar character, the question whether this rule is one of *jus cogens* or may be abrogated by agreements between individual States is rather sterile. No such agreement could affect the duties incumbent on any subject of international law in relation to third parties. Between the contracting parties, any such agreement would mean no more than that they would not demand from each other the institution of criminal proceedings in their own countries against alleged forgers of the other country's currency. Even if the rules on the prohibition of counterfeiting foreign currencies were rules of international *jus cogens*, any State would remain entitled to waive this right. Similarly, if, in relation to a rule in this exalted category, any formal waiver was thought to be inappropriate on grounds of international public policy, a State would always remain free not to take any action at all.

3. *Article 16 of the League Covenant.*

If ever a rule was mandatory, it was paragraph 1 of Article 16 of the Covenant of the League of Nations.[39]

A member of the League which resorts to war contrary to its obligations under Articles 12, 13 or 15 of the Covenant 'shall *ipso facto* be deemed to have committed an act of war against all other members of the League'. These

hereby undertake immediately to subject it to the severance of all trade or financial relations, the prohibitions of all intercourse between their nationals and the nationals of the covenant-breaking State, and the prevention of all financial, commercial or personal intercourse between the nationals of the covenant-breaking State and the nationals of any other State, whether a Member of the League or not.

This clause was open to criticism on the ground that its authors had over-estimated the likely effectiveness of economic sanctions. It was also fair to comment unfavourably on the bad drafting of the prohibition of relations between nationals of the parties involved. The intention was the application not of a national but of a territorial test.

What was not intended was what actually happened: an interpretative resolution, passed with almost indecorous haste in 1921 by the

31

second League assembly. It consisted of a series of recommendations, intended merely for 'guidance', and it was demurely described as a 'provisional measure', pending formal amendments of Article 16 of the Covenant.

No such formal amendments were ever adopted. Nevertheless, the resolution achieved its end. It left the legal obligations of the member States unimpaired. Yet, it made it the 'duty of each member of the League to decide for himself whether a breach of the Covenant has been committed'. Thus it substituted sovereign discretion for automatic international action and, inevitably, weakened the faith in a system of sanctions, operating automatically against any transgressor. It was the beginning of a gradually accelerating process of *de facto* revision of the League Covenant, reaching its crescendo in the years immediately preceding the second world war.

The crucial test which was to make or break the League of Nations came with the Italo-Ethiopian war. No doubt existed on the deliberate preparation and execution of the Italian design for aggression. Non-universality never mattered less than at that moment in the whole history of the League of Nations. The Soviet Union had become a member of the League, and the United States of America showed sympathetic interest in the contemplated League action. Even Nazi Germany adopted a policy of cautious but watchful neutrality.

Actually, the leading members of the League were impeded by two overriding fears. They did not wish to deprive themselves of what they thought was Mussolini's restraining influence on Hitler. Even more, they dreaded the spectre of Communism in Europe if the Fascist regime in Italy should collapse as the result of too successful an experiment with League sanctions.

Thus, while Italy leisurely and publicly prepared for action, the League Secretariat made no preparations for the imminent contingency. If, with Fascist members on its staff, it was difficult for the Secretariat to take such action, the member States, which were familiar with these difficulties, failed to make concerted alternative arrangements. When the aggression took place they left matters with a hastily established committee of co-ordination, reminiscent of diplomatic conferences in pre-1914 style.

The members of the League did not, as provided in the Covenant, subject Italy 'immediately' to the 'severance of all trade or financial relations'; they did not prohibit 'all intercourse' between persons resident in their countries and that of the covenant-breaking State, nor prevent 'all financial, commercial or personal intercourse' between residents in the 'covenant-breaking State' and in 'any other State whether a member of the League or not'.

Similarly, the League Council did nothing to implement the complementary duty incumbent upon it under Article 16 of the Covenant. It failed to 'recommend' to the several governments concerned what 'effective military, naval or air force the Members of the League shall severally contribute to the armed forces to be used to protect the covenants of the League'.

The League members brought economic sanctions into operation, but haltingly, gradually and piecemeal. The United Kingdom and France had made it clear that in no circumstances were they prepared to apply military sanctions against Italy. Thus they made an unexpected contribution to the definition of sanctions in the repertory of the League of Nations: a military sanction was any action, including economic sanctions, which happened to inconvenience the aggressor, and against which he threatened to take military counter-measures. As this contingency was to be avoided at all costs, the decision on the dividing line between economic and military sanctions passed to the aggressor. Mussolini lost no time in making it clear that he would treat the, to him, highly inconvenient and probably disastrous oil sanction (especially if coupled with a closure of the Suez Canal) as a military sanction and respond to it with suitable military counter-measures. Therefore, this economic sanction was never applied.

The fate of Article 16 of the Covenant and the application of sanctions in the Italo-Ethiopian war suggest four lessons:

(i) If economic sanctions are to be decisive, they must be backed by willingness to let their application escalate, if necessary, into the use of all available means of pressure, and this includes military sanctions.

(ii) It is difficult, if not impossible, for any international secretariat on a level of low international integration to engage in competent contingency planning against any member State even when merely economic sanctions are involved.

33

(iii) Irrespective of any legal formulation, any contemplated automatism of concerted economic action which may conflict with vital political interests of leading members of an international confederation is likely to be so re-interpreted as not to interfere unduly with the freedom of action of the 'dispensers', rather than the 'consumers', of international security.

(iv) The failure of sanctionist States to share effectively—as had been envisaged in Paragraph 3 of Article 16 of the League Covenant—the losses and inconveniences resulting from the application of non-military sanctions is likely to impede materially the success of any such experiment.[40]

III. AN INTERIM BALANCE SHEET

Before proceeding to the last stages of the present enquiry—the problem of an economic world order in the post-1945 world and the assessment of the major current trends relevant from this point of view—it may be helpful to summarise the conclusions reached so far.

1. In this as in other branches of international law, pre-1914 unorganised international society provided speculative minds with splendid opportunities to enrich the doctrine of international law with normative pseudo-orders. As might be expected, natural-law ideologies were fully exploited to this end.

2. Viewed from the angle of the dialectic relation between freedom and order, a comparison of the two phases of the evolution of international economic law examined yields a possibly unexpected result. No basic differences exist between the states reached in unorganised international society and international society organised in the League of Nations. What is much more pronounced is the element of continuity. It is indicative of the low degree of integration demanded from and attainable in a loose confederation such as the League of Nations.

3. As in other branches of international law, evidence is lacking during the periods under discussion of any *jus cogens* other than on a consensual basis. In particular, relevant rules of international criminal law are limited to internationally postulated rules of municipal criminal law.

4. Such little consensual *jus cogens* as, in the pre-1914 and 1919–39

34

periods, was superimposed on international economic customary law was too limited and too fragmentary to constitute an international economic order in any meaningful use of the term. In any case, this consensual law fell so far short of universality as hardly to qualify as a world order.

5. The chief significance for our own age of the failure of the sanctions experiment in the Italo-Ethiopian war appears to lie in the lessons it offers on the primacy of politics over economics in any international environment in which, ultimately, power reigns supreme.

6. Whoever may find the conclusions reached in these lectures too harsh has an easy alternative open to him. All he has to do is to lower to his heart's content the standards postulated at the outset of this course for an international order, economic or otherwise. Yet any such game of escapism can be played only at a price. It is to be jerked back to reality, as were previous generations in 1914 and 1939.

NOTES

[1] Ottawa Agreements Act, 1932 (22 and 23 Geo. 5, Ch. 53).

[2] Publications of the Court, Series A/B, No. 42, p. 108, at p. 117 *et seq.* See also M. Hill, *The Economic and Financial Organization of the League of Nations* (1946).

[3] M. O. Hudson, *International Legislation*, Vol. 3, p. 2010.

[4] Martens, 2 N.R.G. (1st ser.), p. 432. See also United Nations, *The Suppression of Slavery*, p. 3 *et seq.* (1951 XIV.2).

[5] Martens, 16 N.R.G. (2nd ser.), p. 3. For the I.L.O. Convention of 28 June 1930 concerning Forced or Compulsory Labour, see M. O. Hudson, *International Legislation*, Vol. 5, p. 609 *et seq.* For relevant statistics on the Convention, see E. A. Landy, *The Effectiveness of International Supervision* (1966), p. 64 *et seq.*, and 232 *et seq.* See also Lord Hailey, *An African Survey* (1945), p. 608 *et seq.*, and below, Chapter IV.

[6] M. O. Hudson, *International Legislation*, Vol. 1, p. 726.

[7] *Ibid.*, Vol. 6, p. 469.

[8] 32 Martens, N.R.G. (2nd ser.), p. 160; 7 *ibid.* (3rd ser.), p. 252.

[9] 7 Martens, N.R.G. (3rd ser.), p. 266. See also below, note 26.

[10] M. O. Hudson, *International Legislation*, Vol. 2, p. 1051. See also below, note 26.

[11] 8 L.N.T.S., p. 187.

[12] M. O. Hudson, *International Legislation*, Vol. 7, p. 359. See, further, B. A. Renborg, *International Drug Control* (1947), p. 220 *et seq.*, and J. G. Starke, *Studies in International Law* (1965), p. 31 *et seq.*

[13] Article 12—English translation of the text in H. P. Willis, *A History of the Latin Monetary Union* (1901), pp. 279–80. See also below, note 27.

[14] M. O. Hudson, *International Legislation*, Vol. 4, p. 2692. See also E. Fitz-Maurice, Convention for the Suppression of Counterfeiting Currency, 26 A.J.I.L. (1932), p. 533 *et seq.*

[15] D. H. Miller, *The Drafting of the Covenant*, Vol. I (1928), p. 172, and below, Appendix 1.

[16] Miller, *loc. cit.*, in note 15, pp. 288–9.

[17] *Ibid.*, p. 259. See below, Appendix 1.

[18] See below, Appendix 1.

[19] Martens, 16 N.R.G. (2nd ser.), p. 3.

[20] 2 Martens N.R.G. (3rd ser.), p. 711.

[21] M. O. Hudson, *International Legislation*, Vol. 1, p. 323. For the reasons why the United States of America refused to ratify the Convention, see A. J. Toynbee, *Survey of International Affairs 1920–1923* (1925), pp. 391–2.

[22] M. O. Hudson, *International Legislation*, Vol. 3, p. 1634. See also the Treaty of 21 August 1930 for the Regulation of the Importation into Ethiopia of Arms, Ammunition and Implements of War, *ibid.*, Vol. 5, p. 723 *et seq.*

[23] See, further, C. Loosli-Usteri, *Geschichte der Konferenz für die Herabsetzung und die Begrenzung der Rüstungen 1932–1934* (1940), p. 467 *et seq.*

[24] See, further, G. O. W. Mueller and E. M. Wise (eds.), *International Criminal Law* (1965), p. 4 *et seq.*

[25] See below, Chapter IV.

[26] The denunciation by Denmark of the 1923 Convention on the Suppression of the Traffic in Obscene Publications (16 August 1967) is significant.

[27] See, however, the cautious formulation of Article 12 of the Treaty of 5 November 1878 between the members of the Latin Monetary Union (*loc. cit.*, p. 35, note 12.

[28] 2 Giff. (1861), p. 628.

[29] *Ibid.*, at p. 678.

[30] *Ibid.*, at p. 679.

[31] *Ibid.*, at p. 679.

[32] 3 De G. F. and J., p. 217, at p. 240.

[33] *Ibid.*, at p. 245 *et seq.*

[34] 120 U.S. 479.

[35] 24 Stats. at L. 22, sections 3 and 6.

[36] Art. I, section 8, cl. 10.

[37] Bk. I, ch. X, para. 108.

[38] See above, pp. 26–7.

[39] See below, Appendix 1.

[40] See also the draft convention of 2 October 1930 on Financial Assistance (M. O. Hudson, *International Legislation*, Vol. 5, p. 751 *et seq.*). According to Article 32, 'it shall be a condition of the entry into force of the present Convention that the ratifications or accessions which it has received shall have resulted in causing a sum of not less than 50 million gold francs, for the annual service of loans, to be covered by ordinary guarantees and also by the special guarantees of not less than three governments' (*ibid.*, p. 774). Beyond this, under Article 35, the entry into force of the Convention was made conditional on the entry into force, in respect of the party concerned, of a plan for the restriction of armaments under Article 8 of the Covenant of the League of Nations (*ibid.*, p. 776). By 1 June 1935 ratifications of the Convention had been deposited by Denmark, Finland and Iran. See also B. Broms, *Finland and the League of Nations* (1963), pp. 92–3, and below, Chapter IV.

Chapter IV

THE PROBLEM OF ECONOMIC WORLD ORDER IN THE UNITED NATIONS ERA

If a quantitative test were significant, the Charter of the United Nations would constitute a considerable advance over the League of Nations in the movement towards an international economic order.

In the League Covenant economic matters were condensed into a single article. In the United Nations Charter two whole chapters and eighteen articles of the Charter are devoted to international economic and social co-operation and to the co-ordination of these activities by the Economic and Social Council of the United Nations. Beyond this, in the scheme of the Charter, the more technical and detailed work is left with Specialised Agencies, entrusted with 'wide international responsibilities' and intended to be co-ordinated by the Economic and Social Council of the United Nations.

I. OBJECTIVES

In the Preamble of the Charter, the promotion of social progress and better standards of life in larger freedom is set out as one of the four chief objectives of the United Nations. The employment of international machinery for furthering the economic and social advancement of all peoples is envisaged as an appropriate means to this end.

Among the purposes of the United Nations is listed international co-operation for the solution of international economic problems. The function of the Organisation is described as that of a centre for harmonising the actions of nations in attaining this and other enumerated common ends.

The object of Chapter IX of the Charter, which is concerned with international economic and social co-operation, is to formulate these economic and social goals in more concrete terms than was considered advisable in the Preamble and Chapter I.

In Article 55 the ultimate ends of economic and social co-operation are defined as peaceful and friendly relations among nations, based on respect for the principles of equal rights and self-determination of peoples.[1]

To achieve these long-range objectives, conditions of stability and well-being are to be created. Economic and social means of attaining these intermediate aims are the promotion of higher standards of living, full employment, and conditions of economic and social progress and development, as well as the solution of, among others, economic and social problems.

II. THE DESIGN OF THE CHARTER

In scope, the objectives of economic and social co-operation set out in the Charter of the United Nations are wide and important enough to qualify as potential heads of an international economic order. Whether they are intended to be so understood depends on a simple test: the constitutional and legal devices provided for giving them this status.

The responsibility for the discharge of the economic and social functions of the United Nations rests primarily with the General Assembly and, under its authority, with the Economic and Social Council. The functions of these organs are, however, essentially deliberative and policy-initiating or pre-legislative, to use a felicitous term recently employed by the President of the International Court of Justice.[2] If any of these activities are in the field of decision-making at all, they are rather peripheral.[3] Although, elsewhere in the Charter, the Economic and Social Council is described as a principal organ of the United Nations, actually it is subordinate to the General Assembly.

Only in the most general terms have the members of the United Nations pledged themselves in Article 56 of the Charter, to take joint and separate action in co-operation with the Organisation for the achievement of the purposes set out in Article 55 of the Charter.[4] Yet the United Nations itself is not able to take any action in these fields. It may merely pass resolutions, recommending action to member States, promote relevant studies and research, or convene conferences concerned with the drafting of conventions for the consideration of member States. Thus members are under no legal obligation to implement any specific recommendation or draft convention.

If Article 56 is not completely meaningless—a result of legal interpretation which should be avoided—it may be considered as a reaffirmation of the principle of good faith, embodied in more general terms in paragraph 2 of Article 2 of the Charter of the United Nations. There may also be implied in this article a duty of the governments of member States to submit relevant draft conventions, initiated by the United Nations, to their own national organs for approval or implementation under their own municipal laws. Yet the duties of good faith incumbent under international customary law on parties to treaties fall but little short of any such implied obligations.

The attempts made to coax water out of this rather stony article are not—and hardly can be—impressive. The reason for this emerges from the drafting history of the article. Its object was to gloss over a far-reaching difference of opinion that had arisen at the San Francisco conference of 1945.

The Australian delegation had proposed an additional article which would have given more concrete meaning to the pledges given in Article 56. According to this draft, the members of the United Nations were to report annually to the General Assembly on the action they had taken to implement the economic and social objectives of the United Nations and recommendations of the Economic and Social Council. The delegation of the United States of America feared that this proposal would make too large an inroad into economic sovereignty. The formulation adopted served to cover up this discord.[5]

III. THE PRACTICE OF ECONOMIC AND SOCIAL CO-OPERATION IN THE UNITED NATIONS

The apparatus of the Economic and Social Council of the United Nations does not err on the side of simplicity. It has an infrastructure of nine functional and three regional commissions. These are served by a plethora of sub-commissions, standing committees, *ad hoc* committees and special bodies.

The results attained are the only fair test of this apparent hyper-trophy. To the extent to which they lie in the fields of policy initiation and co-ordination, they are outside the purview of our inquiry. What we are concerned with is to find evidence of procedures for the creation of mandatory legal rules or economic *jus cogens* on this near-universal level.

In performing this task of evaluation, undue rigidity must be avoided. It does not matter how consensus on such law evolves. What matters is whether, in fact, legal rules of such an international economic order have come into existence.

From this angle, three facets of the activities of the United Nations are more likely than others to yield positive results:

1. Relevant resolutions of the Economic and Social Council and the General Assembly of the United Nations.
2. The practice of the United Nations in the application of sanctions, in particular economic sanctions.
3. Relevant multilateral conventions.

1. *Resolutions*

In principle, the purely advisory character of the General Assembly of the United Nations, and *a fortiori* the Economic and Social Council as one of its subsidiary organs, prevents the resolutions of these bodies from having any automatically binding effect. There are exceptions to this rule. Yet in the context of these lectures they are, at the most, peripheral. They are based either on express pro-visions of the Charter, such as those on the exercise of budgetary powers, or they are concerned with the fulfilment of other internal functions of the United Nations by the General Assembly, or with the creation of further auxiliary bodies, such as the United Nations Development Programme.

This does not exclude that affirmations and assertions, contained in resolutions of any of these organs and purporting to be declara-tory of existing international law, and of statements that individual rules constitute international *jus cogens*, may become legally binding on member States in other ways. In particular, this may be the result of estoppels, created, for instance, by concurrence in particular resolutions or by silence in circumstances in which, in good faith, a protest, a reservation of rights or some other form of dissent may be expected.

It must suffice to select among other possibly relevant resolutions that on Permanent Sovereignty over Natural Resources, adopted by the General Assembly on 15 December 1962.[6] It may claim preference on at least five grounds. For a decade the subject was before the General Assembly, the Economic and Social Council and a special commission established in 1958 by the General Assembly. It was thoroughly studied by the United Nations Secretariat. The 1962 resolution was adopted with near-unanimity, including the votes of the major capital-exporting States except France. It was re-affirmed in 1966, this time with no vote against it, but with Japan, the United Kingdom and the United States of America joining the abstainers.[7] Finally, especially in Communist countries and those of the 'third world', the principles enunciated and reiterated in a whole series of further resolutions adopted by the General Assembly on permanent sovereignty over natural resources tend to be treated as international *jus cogens*.

In analysing the resolution it appears fairest to adopt the working hypothesis that the resolution is a legally relevant document. Thus the first task is to explore whether it adds anything to international law as it stands.

In this work of interpretation, it is necessary to bear in mind six points made in the preamble of the resolution:

(i) The 'status' of permanent sovereignty over natural wealth and resources is viewed as a 'basic constituent of the right to self-determination'.

(ii) The General Assembly bears in mind a recommendation it had passed earlier that the sovereign right of every State to dispose of its wealth and natural resources should be respected, and considers that any such measure of disposal must be based on recognition of the 'inalienable' right of all States freely to dispose of their natural wealth and resources in accordance with their national interest, and on respect for the economic independence of States.

(iii) It is recognised that Principle 4, enunciated in the resolution, is not to prejudice the position of any member State on any

41

aspect of the question of the rights and obligations of successor States and governments regarding property acquired before the accession to complete sovereignty of countries formerly under colonial rule.

(iv) The General Assembly considers that economic and financial agreements between developed and developing countries must be based on the principles of equality and the right of peoples and nations to self-determination.

(v) The provision of economic and technical assistance, loans and increased foreign investment must not be subject to conditions which conflict with the interests of recipient States.

(vi) The General Assembly notes that the creation and strengthening of the inalienable sovereignty of States over their internal wealth and resources reinforce their economic independence.

The substance of the resolution is embodied in eight Principles. They can be conveniently examined in the form of commentaries attached to a textual reproduction of each of these Principles.

1. *'The right of peoples and nations to permanent sovereignty over their natural wealth and resources must be exercised in the interest of their national development and of the well-being of the people of the State concerned.'*

This Principle may be taken as an exhortation addressed to the authorities of all States, in particular the members of the United Nations, on the spirit in which they ought to exercise their governmental functions. If this Principle were meant to be understood as a mandatory rule of international law, it would transform the proper exercise of this trust into a matter of international concern and take it out of the preserve of matters which, by paragraph 7 of Article 2 of the Charter, are essentially under the domestic jurisdiction of any sovereign State. It may be assumed that it was not the intention of the General Assembly to reach this conclusion. The only alternative appears to be to treat this Principle as lacking any legal meaning.

2. *'The exploration, development and disposition of such resources, as well as the import of the foreign capital required for these purposes, should be in conformity with the rules and conditions which the peoples*

42

and nations freely consider to be necessary or desirable with regard to the authorisation, restriction or prohibition of such activities.'

In principle, contracts for the exploration, development and disposition of natural wealth and resources are public contracts under municipal law. In the absence of evidence of any contrary intention of the contracting parties, they are subject to the municipal law of the host State.

Even if this is taken for granted, four questions arise regarding the 'free' decision on the necessity or desirability of the authorisation, restriction or prohibition of such activities:

First, do the words chosen mean that any *de facto* or *de jure* government of an independent State is entitled to represent the 'peoples' and 'nations' in making their free decision? In this case, the voices of a great many peoples and nations in member States of the United Nations are likely to remain unheard. If not, Principle 2 would have revolutionary implications.

Second, at which particular time is this 'free' assessment to be made? The benefits to be derived from a public contract tend to look more attractive to a host State before than after a foreign investment has been made.

Third, does the juxtaposition of authorisation, restriction and prohibition mean that a freely granted authorisation may be subsequently restricted or turned into a prohibition? If so, this freedom is limited by Principle 4 of the resolution.[8]

Fourth, who is to decide on whether the condition of 'free' consideration is fulfilled? In the absence of agreement on third-party adjudication between the parties to a public contract, the only contribution to the issue made by the resolution is the introduction of a further element of potential dissent.[9]

3. *'In cases where authorisation is granted, the capital imported and the earnings on that capital shall be governed by the terms thereof, by the national legislation in force, and by international law. The profits derived must be shared in the proportions freely agreed upon, in each case, between the investors and the recipient State, due care being taken to ensure that there is no impairment, for any reason, of that State's sovereignty over its natural wealth and resources.'*

In the first sentence, the hierarchy in ascending order of the legal rules applicable to public contracts is correctly stated.

43

That profits from capital imports must be shared as agreed, may be thought to be self-understood. Yet again, who decides on whether the agreement was freely made?

The three revisions of the Oil Consortium Agreement of 1954, between Iran and the National Iranian Oil Company as the first parties and the companies forming the Iranian Oil Consortium of 1954 as the second parties, illustrate the relativity of freedom on both sides in typical relations of interdependence between foreign operators and a host State. The latter has the local monopoly in particular natural resources, and the fixed assets of the oil companies under its jurisdiction are subject to its control. Moreover, it may be taken that the exploitation of these assets is profitable, and the potentialities of the exploitation areas are valuable to the investor, if only for the purpose of denying them to a rival. The other side of the coin is the large-scale control of world market facilities by the foreign oil companies, the accelerating depreciation of fixed assets such as oil installations in an age of fast technological change, the technical know-how at the disposal of these companies, the abundance of oil on a world scale and the discount on oil east of Suez. Thus, who may be considered to be free—and how far— appear to be philosophical, rather than legal, questions.

In cases other than those of force, duress, fraud or imposition on groups of persons singled out for special protection through immaturity or infirmity, even highly mature systems of municipal law must work on the assumption of freedom. This is why not even abstractions from pertinent rules of municipal law in the form of a general principle of law recognised by civilised nations would carry matters any further.[10]

The non-impairment of a State's sovereignty—the last of the *desiderata* of Principle 3—by a public contract can be discussed on levels of form and substance.

In form, any public contract is an exercise and, thus, an affirmation of national sovereignty. This reasoning was cogently employed by the Permanent Court of International Justice in the *Wimbledon* case (1923) for the purpose of disposing of allegedly inalienable rights of German sovereignty.[11] It applies no less to public contracts under municipal law than to engagements under international law.[12]

In substance, legal domination of a small country by foreign companies and governments can easily reach a point when the sovereignty of the 'host' State is reduced to a mere shadow. The activities of the United Fruit Company in Central America prior to the inauguration of F. D. Roosevelt's good neighbour policy, the joint companies established during the Stalinist period for 'co-operation' between the Soviet Union and each of its European allies—and, inevitably, providing for Russian majority holdings—and multinational companies are to the point.

On a basis of common sense, it is always possible to find a golden mean between such extremes. Yet, when a successor government in a host country looks through a magnifying glass at 'freely' negotiated agreements of any of its predecessors in office, it is likely to find them wanting. Even if a dispute on this matter were to be settled by arbitration under the 1965 Convention on the Settlement of Investment Disputes between States and Nationals of other States, any decision would contain so many subjective elements that the all-important question would always be the person chosen as the umpire in a three-member tribunal.[13]

4. *'Nationalisation, expropriation or requisitioning shall be based on grounds or reasons of public utility, security or the national interest which are recognised as overriding purely individual interest, both domestic and foreign. In such cases the owner shall be paid appropriate compensation, in accordance with the rules in force in the State taking such measures in the exercise of its sovereignty and in accordance with international law. In any case where the question of compensation gives rise to a controversy, the national jurisdiction of the State taking such measures shall be exhausted. However, upon agreement by sovereign States and other parties concerned, settlement of the dispute should be made through arbitration or international adjudication.'*

In the first sentence of Principle 4, the rule of international customary law, permitting expropriation in the public interest as an exception to the prohibition of interference with foreign-owned property, is verbosely restated.

The formulation 'appropriate' compensation leaves uncertain whether this term is to be equated with full or partial compensation. Thus, it leaves the existing controversy on this issue unresolved.[14]

The whole emphasis regarding the manner in which compensation is to be paid is put on the law of the expropriating State. In some

45

cases—as, for instance, when a foreign national is resident there—this is likely to constitute effective compensation, as demanded by international customary law. In other cases—as, for instance, the payment into a blocked account of compensation owed to a non-resident foreign national—this mode of payment would run counter to the effectivity rule. In all cases, the test is the governing rule of international customary law, and not the national law of any of the States involved.

The restatement of the need for the exhaustion of local remedies prior to making an international claim regarding inadequate compensation is in accordance with international customary law. The formulation is, however, too wide. It does not allow for the exceptions to the rule when local remedies need not be exhausted because, in law or fact, they do not exist and, therefore, cannot be exhausted.

To suggest that, *if the parties agree*, a dispute on compensation should be settled through arbitration or international adjudication is a splendid example of stating the obvious in as many as twenty-two words.

5. '*The free and beneficial exercise of the sovereignty of peoples and nations over their natural resources must be furthered by the mutual respect of States based on their sovereign equality.*'

Suffice it to note that, in this case, thirty words were required for a further platitudinous exercise.

6. '*International co-operation for the economic development of developing countries, whether in the form of public or private capital investment, exchange of goods and services, technical assistance, or exchange of scientific information, shall be such as to further their independent national development and shall be based upon respect for their sovereignty over their natural wealth and resources.*'

In a world community, this Principle could be conceived as a directive of international public policy, applied by international governmental, administrative, and judicial organs. In the Disunited Nations, rules formulated as broadly as Principle 6 tend to be used as additional ammunition in campaigns of mutual denigration. They offer para-legal rules by reference to which one can condemn with equal ease United States economic 'hegemonism' in the western hemisphere and 'limited sovereignty', as re-imposed by the Soviet Union on Czechoslovakia.

7. '*Violation of the rights of peoples and nations to sovereignty over their natural wealth and resources is contrary to the spirit and principles of the Charter of the United Nations and hinders the development of international co-operation and the maintenance of peace.*'

If the 'rights' mentioned in Principle 7 were spelled out in more concrete terms, it would be easier to give some meaning to this Principle. Similarly, if 'peoples and nations' merely meant sovereign States or member States of the United Nations, it might be advisable to say so. Otherwise, Biafrans, Somalis and others who consider themselves to be unjustly deprived of their own right to self-determination might be led to believe that these Principles might operate one day also in their favour.

8. '*Foreign investment agreements freely entered into by or between sovereign States shall be observed in good faith. States and international organisations shall strictly and conscientiously respect the sovereignty of peoples and nations over their natural wealth and resources in accordance with the Charter and the principles set forth in the present resolution*'.

This Principle is intended to restore a balance in a resolution so far overweighted against capital-exporting States. Otherwise, it would hardly be required to restate that international investment agreements and public contracts should be observed in good faith. That it should be necessary to affirm this proposition at all is some further indication of what foreign investors have to expect in the majority of capital-importing States. In addition, the limitation of this obligation to agreements entered 'freely' raises all the doubts voiced on this matter in connection with Principles 2, 3 and 5.

The resolution in perspective. At first sight, it may be hard to understand why so much attention should be paid to so verbose and obscure an exercise in resolution-mongering.

On further reflection, this very character of the resolution is perhaps its chief attraction. It enables representatives of capital-importing States to point to a document agreed on with representatives of the chief capital-exporting States in which a number of crucial points appear to have been conceded by implication. For instance, only *freely* concluded investment agreements require to be observed in good faith, and everybody is free to decide for himself whether any particular agreement complies with this requisite.

47

Similarly, it is arguable that *appropriate* compensation in cases of nationalisation, expropriation or requisition falls short of full (or adequate), effective and prompt compensation as postulated by international customary law.[15]

Conversely, representatives of capital-exporting States may claim that, by definition, any agreement concluded with any of the new— sovereign and equal—members of the United Nations is freely concluded. Thus, it may be hopefully thought that, at last, these elusive partners have been tied down to the acceptance of some reasonable standards in international economic relations. Some Western operators might even consider that if these rules were not completely satisfactory and fell below those of international customary law, this state of affairs was preferable to one of complete lawlessness and irresponsibility.

At least among themselves, the present-day beneficiaries of the principle of the self-determination of peoples might do well to discuss a nightmare of their own. Their particular problems as heirs of multi-national empires are the self-perpetuating character of the potent but explosive principle of the self-determination of peoples and their fear of peoples and nations in these sovereign States longing to apply these principles against their new and non-white masters. The juggling in the resolution with the apparently interchangeable terms 'sovereign States', 'peoples' and 'nations' bears witness to these well grounded anxieties.

Moreover, nothing could have been worse from the point of view of capital-importing States than an affirmation in legally binding form of the principle of the inalienable character of sovereignty over natural wealth and resources. The principle would have implied a total incapacity of the governments of States which have little to offer foreign investors except natural resources and wealth in exchange for capital and technological know-how to conclude binding agreements under international or municipal law. Thus it would have destroyed the last vestiges of their rather relative creditworthiness.

All concerned shied away from taking any such extreme line and contented themselves with the application of a technique in vogue since the days of the naturalist doctrine of international law. While, in principle, sovereignty is inalienable, it is alienable in certain circumstances and, in the context of the resolution, these are defined as those of freely negotiated agreements.

If our world were dominated by capital-exporting States, naturalist ideologists might have elevated into absolute principles other principles more to their liking, such as that of *Pacta sunt servanda*, to justify the need for the faithful execution of any investment agreement, and this is exactly what, in the past, Western company lawyers excelled in doing. In an international society divided into world blocs, with the 'third world' forming an uneasy and unstable in-between area, the naturalist ideology of inalienable sovereignty over natural wealth and resources is not intended to constitute a new rule of consensual *jus cogens*. It is no more than a convenient para-legal ideology of power economics.

2. *Economic sanctions in United Nations practice*

According to Article 41 of the Charter of the United Nations, the Security Council may decide, *inter alia*, on measures not involving the use of armed force to give effect to its decisions under Chapter VII of the Charter. It may also call upon the members of the United Nations to apply such measures. These may include the complete or partial interruption of economic and diplomatic relations and all forms of communication with the State against which sanctions are applied.

Prior to the Rhodesian sanctions experiment, the United Nations made several half-hearted efforts on the fringes and in the field of economic sanctions.

In three of these cases—those of Spain, Portugal and South Africa —the Western members of the Security Council were less than enthusiastic. In that of Korea, after temporarily absenting itself, the Soviet Union blocked further action. Thus in each case it was left to the General Assembly to fill the gaps as best it could. Actually, this meant that members of the United Nations willing to take individual action could rely on some United Nations authority, however spurious.

In 1946 the General Assembly recommended to the member States to withdraw the heads of their diplomatic missions from Madrid. It rejected a proposal of the Soviet Union and her allies to recommend the application of economic sanctions against Spain.

On the intiative of a number of Latin American States, the General Assembly rescinded its resolution in 1950 and thus put an end to this ill-conceived half-measure.

In 1951 the General Assembly recommended, under the Uniting for Peace resolution of 1950,[16] an embargo on the export of a series of materials useful for purposes of war to Communist China and North Korea. Yet these economic measures were merely ancillary to the military efforts made under United Nations auspices to assist Southern Korea.

After the Korean armistice of 1953, the Western Powers continued economic measures against China and North Korea in the shape of strategic trade embargoes under the aegis of Chincom, a committee of NATO Powers and Japan. This was the twin of Cocom, a corresponding committee concerned with Western trade with the Soviet bloc. As the Cocom list was less stringent than that of Chincom, the effect was to put a premium on Western trade with China via Eastern Europe and the Soviet Union.[17]

On the level of the United Nations, probably the most significant result of its involvement in the Korean war was the establishment of a Collective Measures Committee by the General Assembly. Yet its recommendations to strengthen the capability of the United Nations to maintain peace remained still-born.

In the years between 1961 and 1965 the General Assembly passed a series of resolutions recommending the application of economic sanctions against Portugal.[18] The object was to induce Portugal to apply the principle of self-determination to its African colonies. The Security Council limited itself to passing in 1963 and 1965 equally Platonic resolutions, recommending a ban on war materials useful to Portugal in her colonial wars in Africa.

Similarly, in 1962 the General Assembly recommended applying diplomatic and economic sanctions against the Republic of South Africa.[19] This resolution was adopted against the votes of the United States, Japan and the 'white' members of the Commonwealth, with the Scandinavian and Latin American countries abstaining.

In 1963, the Security Council found that the situation in South Africa was seriously disturbing international peace and security, and called upon all States to stop the sale of war materials to the Republic of South Africa. France and the United Kingdom abstained. They associated themselves, however, with a subsequent resolution of the Security Council, passed during the same year and strengthening the previous resolution on the arms embargo. In doing so, they drew a distinction between arms destined for external defence, which they would continue to export to South Africa, and others to be employed for purposes of internal suppression which they would cease to supply. After the Labour victory in the 1964 election, the United Kingdom government banned all exports of arms to South Africa.[20]

In 1964, the Security Council established a Committee of Experts for the study of the feasibility, effectiveness and implications of sanctions against the Republic of South Africa. The committee's report was published in 1965, disclosing a majority of six to four against the application of economic sanctions. While the General Assembly continued to call for economic sanctions against the Republic of South Africa, in fact nothing further happened. The relative economic invulnerability of South Africa, the lure of South African gold, the value of South African bases in Western global strategy, and the expenses of an oil embargo, supported by a maritime blockade and covering the neighbouring Portuguese colonies, made militant proposals directed against South Africa less than attractive to those primarily called upon to shoulder these burdens.[21]

Against this unpromising background, the application of economic sanctions against Rhodesia may sound astonishing. To understand the peculiarities and, therefore, relative insignificance of these measures from the point of view of international economic order, it is essential to bear in mind eleven salient aspects:

(a) At the time of Rhodesia's unilateral declaration of independence in 1965 the United Kingdom was under its own constitutional law and under international law, if hardly any longer in fact, responsible for Rhodesia.

(b) Already prior to this Rhodesian act of open defiance, the United Kingdom government had announced that in no circumstances would it apply military sanctions against Rhodesia.[22]

(c) Following Rhodesia's unilateral declaration of independence, the United Kingdom took voluntarily such limited legislative, administrative and economic action against Rhodesia as, from London, it was able to take.

(d) Simultaneously, the Security Council of the United Nations

51

urged all States to cease to supply the Salisbury government with military material and to break economic relations with Rhodesia, in particular to stop the export of oil and oil products to Rhodesia.[23]

(e) In 1966, at the request of the United Kingdom, the Security Council authorised the United Kingdom under Article 39 of the Charter to intercept ships bound for Beira and suspect of carrying oil with Rhodesia as the destination.[24]

(f) After the failure of the talks on H.M.S. *Tiger* in December 1966, the United Kingdom government asked the Security Council for the imposition of mandatory economic sanctions against Rhodesia. The measures decided on by the Security Council fell short, however, of the sanctions already voluntarily applied by the United Kingdom and a number of other countries. It was not until 1968 that, at least on paper, the Security Council closed the existing loopholes.[25] The Security Council failed, however, to establish a compensation fund for more than average losses suffered by particular sanctionist States.[26]

(g) The Rhodesian sanctions experiment differs in its object from the application of sanctions by the League of Nations against Italy. While, in the latter case, sanctions were to lead to the abandonment of external aggression, in the former it is to induce a return to a previous constitutional status and, possibly, agreement of the white minority to black majority rule in the foreseeable future.

Even so, the two experiments have two features in common: the inability or unwillingness of some sanctionist States to make the economic weapon effective and, if necessary, supplement it by the application of force. In both cases the operative factors which imposed these hesitations and limitations sufficed to reduce the application of economic sanctions to an expensive but ineffective demonstration of moral rectitude.

(h) In relation to Rhodesia, neighbouring African States show an understandable but unheroic discretion regarding strong measures, as distinct from strong words.

(i) In 1969 Rhodesia's annual export trade was estimated to amount to about £60 million in contravention of official sanctions policy and £44 million by way of tolerated exceptions, including the export of coal to Zambia.[27]

(j) The techniques of 'sanction-busting' employed are simple:

52

open contravention and false or forged certificates of origin. In particular, Japan, France, Germany and Switzerland have noticeably increased their trade with Rhodesia since comprehensive sanctions started.[28]

(*k*) A retort, more effective than economic and military sanctions, but outside the Charter of the United Nations, is likely to constitute black Rhodesia's miracle weapon against indefinite white domination: the biological weapon. In 1968, Rhodesia had 250,000 white and 4,500,000 black inhabitants. On conservative estimates, respective figures are likely to be, in twenty years' time, 400,000 and 10 million.[29]

Evaluation. The experiments with diplomatic and economic sanctions carried out under the auspices of the United Nations fall into three categories:

(i) Such sanctions may be essentially symbolic or mere window-dressing, as in the case of the diplomatic sanctions applied against Spain.

(ii) They may be flukes, as the action resolved on by the Security Council against China and North Korea during the temporary absence of the Soviet Union, or on the invitation of a State internationally responsible for a particular territory, as the United Kingdom in the case of Rhodesia.

(iii) They may be substitutes for action as primarily envisaged under the Charter. This applied, and applies, to all cases in which the General Assembly made, and makes, recommendations in spheres where, under the Charter, collective action is reserved to the Security Council.

The fact that in the case of Rhodesia the United Kingdom was not able or willing to apply force may partly explain the failure of the application of economic sanctions in this instance. It is not, however, the whole of the story.

In war blockade-running is a well-known phenomenon, and a frequent result of wartime prohibitions of trade is that such trade chooses new routes or that, in the blockaded country, substitute industries come into existence. Wars may even be holy wars, as were the Crusades, and trade with infidels may be interdicted by Popes and Church councils. Yet even then contraband trade between

Christians and Moslems flourished. The splendour of towns such as medieval Ragusa still attests to the success with which such bans were defied.

If this can happen in alliances against common enemies—so far the strongest bond between entities such as sovereign States, which consider themselves to be ultimate values—how much more likely is this to be the fate of collective efforts, limited to economic pressure in states of peace and on levels of fairly modest international integration?

3. *Relevant multilateral treaties*

The multilateral treaties to be considered fall into three groups: conventions in the pre-1914 and League of Nations traditions; new ventures in the codification and development of international economic law, and the efforts made to formulate economic human rights.

(*a*) *A humanitarian tradition continued.* In the fields of immoral traffic in women and children, slavery and dangerous drugs, the United Nations took over where the League of Nations had left these matters.

In 1949 the United Nations adopted a *Convention for the Suppression of the Traffic in Persons and of the Exploitation of the Prostitution of Others*, consolidating earlier conventions and draft conventions. The resolution to which the draft convention was attached was adopted by thirty-four votes to two (France and the United Kingdom), with fifteen abstentions (including the United States of America).[30]

The attempts made in the Convention to widen the scope of relevant criminal acts were less drastic than at first appears. In Article 12 it is provided that the offences referred to in the Convention shall in each State be 'defined, prosecuted and punished in conformity with its domestic law'. Even so, the Convention has been ratified only by a small number of States, primarily Communist and Asian States.

As in some related League of Nations codifications, the position of parties to the Convention on the general question of the limits of criminal jurisdiction under itnernational law is expressly reserved.

On the most charitable interpretation, the reason for the lack of interest in this venture in international law-making is that the problem has ceased to be of an international character. It is supposed to have become an internal question which each State must settle for itself by its passport regulations and other administrative devices. It is more likely that the humanitarian idealism which had prompted the earlier endeavours in this field has exhausted itself, and that those concerned were prepared to accept the differences in national policies and social standards which had come to light in the discussions on the draft convention as amounting to an impossibility of effective joint action on a universalist level.

In the *Supplementary Convention on Slavery* of 7 September 1956 the contracting parties recognised that 'slavery, the slave trade and institutions and practices similar to slavery have not yet been eliminated in all parts of the world'. They concentrated in this instrument on assimilating to slavery related institutions such as forms of debt bondage and serfdom.

Reservations to the Convention are excluded, but any party may denounce it, with effect at the end of one of the successive three-year periods into which the application of the Convention is divided.

The two most significant aspects of the Convention are its omissions. The parties did not grant to one another's naval ships and military aircraft the right of visit and search of ships suspected of engaging in slave trading. More significant, the parties did not, and could not, deal in the framework of the United Nations with forms of serfdom more obnoxious to the 'dignity and worth of the human person' than domestic slavery and serfdom—those inflicted on the whole of their populations by any of the totalitarian and most of the authoritarian States. Yet all those States are eligible to become parties to the Convention.[31]

In the *Single Narcotic Drugs Convention* of 30 March 1961, the United Nations attempted to consolidate the earlier treaties on the subject. Yet the price of trying to achieve wider participation was a considerable relaxation of the standards attained in the 1936 Convention. This applied to the duties of international co-operation laid down in the earlier Convention and the provision made there for the punishment of enumerated offences and the extraditable character of such offences. Thus, a number of States insisted that the 1936 Convention should remain in force side by side with the less far-reaching effort of the United Nations in the control of dangerous drugs.[32]

If these treaties show any common features in contrast to those concluded during the League of Nations era, it is a tendency to pay even greater attention to the susceptibilities of the guardians of national sovereignty by a more cautious formulation of international obligations and further provision for renunciation and escape clauses.

(b) *New ventures*. Eleven multilateral conventions are more likely than others to contain rules which are potentially in the class of an international economic order. Six are concerned with the law of the sea. The Antarctic Treaty is in a category of its own. The other four treaties are intended to regulate consular relations, nuclear explosions other than those carried out underground, the non-proliferation of nuclear weapons and other nuclear explosive devices, and activities in outer space. Again, the examination of these Conventions will be limited to the angles which are especially important from the point of view of a potential international economic order.

The relevant Conventions from the law of the sea are the four Geneva Conventions of 1958 on the Law of the Sea, the 1960 Convention for the Safety of Life at Sea and the 1965 Convention on Transit Trade of Land-locked States. This aspect of international law—like international air and space law—overlaps with international economic law. Yet, in any case of doubt on jurisdictional frontiers, it is probably advisable to err on the side of casting the net too wide.

The most directly relevant articles of the Geneva codification of the law of the sea in 1958 are those on piracy and slavery in the *Convention on the High Seas*.[33] A duty is imposed on all States to co-operate 'to the fullest possible extent' in the repression of piracy on the high seas or in any other place outside the jurisdiction of any State. Yet no duty is imposed on States to seize pirate ships or aircraft. States are merely authorised to take such action. Thus, from the point of view of international public order, matters are left where they stood under international customary law.

Similarly, as under the earlier anti-slave trade conventions, every State is enjoined to adopt effective measures to prevent and punish the transport of slaves in ships authorised to fly its flag and prevent the unlawful use of its flag for that purpose.

If there are reasonable grounds for suspecting that a foreign merchant ship is engaged in the slave trade, a warship is authorised to board her, but merely for purposes of verifying the ship's right to fly her flag. Yet, in the case of a slave ship, no rights corresponding to those of seizing pirate ships or aircraft, arrest of the persons on board and seizure of the property on board the pirate ship are granted to foreign warships.

In accordance with a venerable postulate of the natural-law doctrine of international law, it is affirmed in the 1958 Convention on the High Seas that States having no sea coast should have free access to the sea. Yet, in every case, this right depends on 'common agreement' and 'conformity with existing international conventions'.

In the *Convention on Transit Trade* of 8 July 1965, these rights are elaborated in greater detail.[34] The drafting techniques employed in this Convention are of particular interest. The Convention was drafted at a time when the United Nations Conference on Trade and Development (UNCTAD) made its first impact on the United Nations and its Specialised Agencies. Thus, the eight Principles on the subject, adopted by the first UNCTAD Conference of 1964, were incorporated in full in the Preamble of the Convention.

Even at UNCTAD there were considerably more 'new' States with seaboards than without. Most of them were not only highly sovereignty-conscious but, from long co-existence with their land-locked neighbours, fully aware of the valuable bargaining weapon created by their geographical position.

Thus, it was stressed from the outset in the UNCTAD declaration that the eight Principles adopted were 'inter-related and each principle should be construed in the context of the other principles'. The right of each land-locked State to free access to the sea was recognised as an 'essential principle for the expansion of international trade and economic development'. Land-locked States were to be granted rights of passage in the territorial and internal waters of the transit States on a basis of foreign parity and rights of access to sea ports and the use of the ports of the transit State on a footing of inland parity.

Yet all this was to be done only 'by common agreement' and 'on the basis of reciprocity'. The transit State was to be safeguarded in relation to third parties by exemption of the facilities and rights

57

which it accorded to land-locked States from the operation of the most-favoured-nation standard.

The Convention adds little to the Barcelona Convention and Statute on Freedom of Transit, adopted in 1921 under the auspices of the League of Nations.[35] Even so—not counting the time spent at the preceding UNCTAD conference of 1964—it took thirty-five plenary meetings of the United Nations Conference on Transit Trade of Land-locked Countries to draft the Convention. It is also noteworthy that the Convention contains wider exception clauses than the Barcelona Convention of 1921 in favour of freedom of action regarding national public policy, security interests, emergencies, war, and the rights and duties of contracting parties as members of the United Nations.

Unlike the Barcelona Convention and Statute, the 1965 Convention contains a revision clause, but no denunciation clause. This feature would probably be the only pointer to any intention of the contracting parties to treat the Convention as consensual *jus cogens*.

Perhaps the most impressive efforts towards effective international legislation in contemporary international economic law and related fields are the successive *Conventions for the Safety of Life at Sea* of 1914, 1929, 1948 and 1960.[36]

These conventions grew out of long-standing British practices, national legislation introduced by Great Britain and taken over by other maritime countries, and standards insisted on by Lloyd's as the world's leading underwriters of maritime insurance. From these beginnings, works of increasingly detailed codification emerged, for which the Inter-governmental Maritime Consultative Organisation is now responsible.

Like the complementary Regulations for Preventing Collisions at Sea,[37] the Regulations for the Safety of Life at Sea probably qualify as little inclusion among the rules of an international economic order as corresponding and equally beneficial road codes under municipal law form part of the rules on national public policy. They offer, however, a fair measuring rod for judging claims to this effect of more ambitious projects, reduced in legal significance by undue vagueness or hedged round by far-reaching escape clauses.

So far, the economic significance of Antarctica is potential rather than actual. Moreover, the legal regime established there under the

Antarctic Treaty of 1959[38] is regional in its geographical scope. Yet all States with historical, territorial, military and economic interests are parties to the treaty, and the regime devised has provided a tangible point of departure for constructive thinking on corresponding problems in outer space.[39] Thus, in case of doubt, the treaty deserves to be included in this survey.

Under the treaty, the use of Antarctica is limited to peaceful activities. They include the economic use and exploitation of the region, but any nuclear explosions and the disposal there of radioactive waste are prohibited.[40] Arrangements are also made for consultation on matters of common interest relating to Antarctica, including the preservation and conservation of living resources in the area.[41]

In the Convention, the special interest of eleven countries in Antarctica are recognised: Argentina, Australia, Belgium, Chile, France, Japan, New Zealand, the Republic of South Africa, the Soviet Union, the United Kingdom and the United States of America. These privileged parties are also known as the consortium Powers, the consultative group or the Article IX group. In the Convention special functions of supervision regarding the maintenance and modification of the treaty regime are allocated to these Powers.[42]

The duration of the treaty is unlimited. While Article IX Powers may modify the treaty at any time by unanimous agreement, any other contracting Powers may call a revision conference only thirty years from the entry into force of the treaty.[43] Dissentient minorities are deemed to have withdrawn from the treaty.[44] These arrangements furnish evidence of the desire of the contracting parties to establish the treaty regime on a semi-permanent basis.

So far, the treaty constitutes the high-water mark in institutionalised forms of co-operation between the Soviet Union and the United States in the post-1945 period. A number of factors contributed to the successful outcome of the negotiations on the 1959 treaty. In this way the two major, and northern, world Powers obtained a wide recognition of their claims to a say in the affairs of the deep south, and they succeeded in transforming these aspirations into a legally confirmed status. Beyond this, the other contracting parties agreed, for the duration of the treaty, not to press any exclusive claims of their own in Antarctica and to accept the political and military neutralisation of the area. Moreover, after considerable hesitation,[45] the United States of America accepted the Soviet Union as an equal partner in the venture, and both treated this gesture as an earnest of mutual willingness to explore further, on this basis, the possibilities of a thaw in hardly less icy relations between them nearer home. Finally, both world Powers co-operated in finding a procedure for accession to the treaty by other States which, for all practical purposes, indefinitely precluded China's accession to the treaty.[46]

The aim of the Vienna *Convention on Consular Relations* of 24 April 1963—like that of 18 April 1961 on Diplomatic Relations —is to 'contribute to the development of friendly relations among nations, irrespective of their differing constitutional and social systems'.[47]

The only feature of the Convention which, from the point of view of an international economic order, deserves attention is the absence of any denunciation clause. It shares this omission with the 1961 Convention on Diplomatic Relations and the 1965 Convention on Transit Trade.

In the case of the Convention on Transit Trade, far-reaching exception clauses ensure a wide range of freedom of action to contracting parties. Similarly, the Vienna Conventions of 1961 and 1963 contain safeguards of their own for the protection of national sovereignty: the requirement of *agrément* under the 1961 Convention and the absolute right to declare any accredited member of a foreign diplomatic mission *persona non grata* and, in the 1963 Convention, the need for an exequatur and a corresponding right to declare any consular officer *persona non grata*.

How much the absence of denunciation clauses is related to the political and military insignificance of treaties, rather than their character as *jus cogens*, is confirmed by three treaties which have economic implications but are primarily of a political and military character. They are the treaty of 5 August 1963 on Banning Nuclear Weapon-tests, the treaty, opened for signature on 1 July 1968, on the Non-proliferation of Nuclear Weapons in the Atmosphere, in Outer Space and under Water, and the treaty of 27 January 1967 on Principles governing the Activities of States in the Exploration and Use of Outer Space, including the moon and other celestial bodies.

The 1963 *Treaty on Banning Nuclear Weapon-tests* is not limited to test explosions of nuclear weapons. It also prohibits any other nuclear explosion, including explosions for economic purposes, in the atmosphere, in outer space and under water. It is expressly provided that the treaty is of unlimited duration. Yet, on three months' notice, each party may withdraw from the treaty 'in exercising its national sovereignty' if it decides that extraordinary events, related to the subject matter of the treaty, have jeopardised the 'supreme interests' of its country.[48]

Under the *Non-Proliferation Treaty* of 1 July 1968[49] each nuclear-weapon State party to the treaty undertakes not to transfer to any recipient whatsoever nuclear weapons or other nuclear explosive devices or control over such weapons or explosive devices directly or indirectly. It may also not in any way assist, encourage or induce any non-nuclear-weapon State to manufacture or otherwise acquire nuclear weapons or other explosive devices or control over such weapons or explosive devices.

Non-nuclear-weapon States impose upon themselves corresponding self-denying ordinances. Yet, under Article IV, this does not affect the 'inalienable' right of all the parties to the treaty to develop research, production and use of nuclear energy for peaceful purposes without discrimination and in conformity with the above obligations.

In assessing the significance of the treaty, three points must be borne in mind:

(i) So far, Communist China and France are not parties to the treaty and remain free to supply signatories and non-signatories alike with nuclear devices and know-how of any kind.

(ii) Expert opinion appears to be divided on the significance in practice of the distinction between the prohibition of the non-proliferation of nuclear explosive devices and the freedom, solemnly affirmed in the treaty, to develop research, production and use of nuclear energy for peaceful purposes.

(iii) With three months' advance notice to the other parties and the Security Council of the United Nations, each party may, 'in exercising its national sovereignty', withdraw from the treaty if it decides that extraordinary events related to the

61

subject-matter of the treaty have jeopardised the 'supreme interests' of its country.

In accordance with the 1967 treaty, outer space, the moon and other celestial bodies are excluded from national appropriation by claim of sovereignty, and this may be taken also to exclude appropriation of any of these areas under private law, as distinct from exploitation of the resources of outer space and celestial bodies.

If such activities are carried on by non-governmental agencies, they require authorisation and supervision by the appropriate State party to the treaty.

Any contracting party may give notice of its withdrawal from the treaty one year after its entry into force, with effect one year thereafter.[50]

The short-term withdrawal clauses in these three treaties suggest the inadvisability of treating, as yet, these consensual engagements as part of an international legal order. If, in years to come, the non-use of these denunciation clauses should prove the *de facto* stability of this order, retrospectively a different evaluation may be more appropriate. It may even be that, in hindsight, international lawyers may consider these treaties to have constituted the Archimedean point from which to solve the problem nearer home of a terrestrial international order. It would not have been the first time that an apparently intractable issue was tackled more successfully from the periphery than from any more centrally situated position.

4. *Economic human rights*

A number of economic human rights are enumerated in the *Universal Declaration of Human Rights* (1948). Prominent among these are the right to own property alone and in association with others; protection against arbitrary deprivation of property; the right to work, the right to the free choice of employment, the right to just and favourable conditions of work, the right to protection against unemployment, the right to equal pay for equal work and the right to form and to join trade unions for the protection of one's interests; the right to an adequate standard of living and the right to a 'social and international order' in which, among others, these economic and social rights can be fully realised.[51]

Attempts have been made since the first world war to translate some of these objectives—first formulated in the peace treaties of 1919—into legally binding obligations. For fifty years the International Labour Organisation has been engaged in the task of building up a coherent body of international labour law. An evaluation of this related work belongs, however, more properly to an assessment of the activities of the relevant Specialised Agencies of the United Nations, all of which, in fact if not aspiration, have established, at most, partial economic orders of their own.[52]

It must suffice here to concentrate on a more comprehensive attempt made in the United Nations itself. After an elephantine period of gestation, it brought forth in 1966 an International Covenant on Economic, Social and Cultural Rights.[53]

Most of the social rights enumerated in the Universal Declaration of Human Rights have found their way into this covenant. Gone, however, are the rights to a free choice of employment, to protection against unemployment and to protection against arbitrary deprivation of property. Besides this, developing countries, although enjoined to pay 'due regard to human rights and their national economy'—the one is likely to cancel out the other—are expressly authorised to discriminate against non-nationals. They may determine for themselves 'to what extent they would guarantee the economic rights recognised in the present Covenant to non-nationals'.

The International Covenant on Economic, Social and Cultural Rights—and even more so the accompanying Covenant on Civil and Political Rights—suffers from an inherent self-contradiction. In three places it is mentioned that the Covenant is drafted on the assumption that the countries of all the contracting parties constitute democratic societies or are supposed to develop towards this goal. It may be granted that Western liberal or social democracy is not the only conceivable type of democracy. Yet one thing is certain: totalitarian and most authoritarian regimes do not belong to this category. Thus, the objects of most of the articles embodied in the Covenant are incompatible with the very structure of such systems of 'tyranny and oppression', as they are aptly termed in the Universal Declaration of Human Rights.

These objectives presuppose a minimum of homogeneity which is absent in the United Nations. Thus one of two results is almost predestined: degradation of such community ideals to ideologies or their reduction to irrelevant utopias. What is impossible in so heterogeneous an environment is to transform such economic human rights into rules of a living international economic order.

NOTES

[1] See below, p. 76 *et seq.*

[2] Address to the International Labour Conference, 18 June 1969 (International Court of Justice—*Communiqué* No. 69/10, 1969).

[3] See, for instance, M. M. Whiteman, *Digest of International Law*, Vol. 13 (1968), p. 610 *et seq.*; H. F. van Panhuys and others (eds.), *International Organisation and Integration* (1968), p. 297 *et seq.*, and W. R. Sharp, *The United Nations Economic and Social Council* (1969), p. 47 *et seq.*

[4] See below, Appendix 2.

[5] See, further, United States Government Printing Office, *The United Nations Conference on International Organization. Selected Documents* (1946), p. 628 *et seq.*

[6] Res. 1803—XVII (14 December 1962).

[7] Res. 2158—XXI (25 November 1966).

[8] See below, p. 45.

[9] For a list of symptomatic writings, see the present writer's *Foreign Investments and International Law* (1969), p. 189, note 22.

[10] See, further, *ibid.*, p. 66 *et seq.*

[11] Publications of the Court, Series A, No. 1, p. 25.

[12] See, further, *supra* note 9, p. 5 *et seq.*

[13] See, further, *ibid.*, p. 135 *et seq.*

[14] For relevant literature, see *ibid.*, pp. 3 and 205 *et seq.*

[15] See *ibid.*, p. 3 *et seq.*

[16] Res. 500—V (18 May 1951). See also K. Skubiszewski, 'The application of non-military measures by the General Assembly of the United Nations', 1 *Polish Yearbook of International Law* (1966–7), p. 110 *et seq.*

[17] See, further, S. Strange, 'The strategic trade embargoes', 12 *Year Book of World Affairs* (1958), p. 55 *et seq.*, and, on the partial lifting of the United States embargo on trade with Communist China, *The Times*, 20 December 1969.

[18] See, for instance, R. St J. MacDonald, 'The resort to economic coercion by international political organisations,' 17 *Univ. Toronto L.J.* (1967), p. 85 *et seq.*, and Margaret Doxey, *Economic Sanctions in the International Enforcement Process* (1970), Ch. 7.

[19] Res. 1761—XVII. See, further, A. C. Leiss, *Apartheid and United Nations* (1965), p. 106 *et seq.*

[20] S/53861 (7 August 1963) and S/5471 (12 December 1963).

[21] S/6210 (2 March 1965). See also *Yearbook of the United Nations* (1965) p. 102 *et seq.*, A. S. Minty, *South Africa's Defence Strategy* (1969) and G. Thayer, *The War Business* (1969).

[22] Hansard H. C., Vol. 718, col. 633 (1 November 1965). See, further, J. W. Halderman, 'Some Legal Aspects of Sanctions in the Rhodesian Case', 17 *I.C.L.Q.* (1968), p. 672 *et seq.*

[23] Gen. Ass. Res. 2022—XX (5 November 1965), and Sec. C. Res. 217—1965 (20 November 1965).

[24] Sec. C. Res. 221 (9 April 1966).

[25] Sec. C. Res. 232—1966, (16 December 1966), and Res. 253—1968 (29 May 1968).

[26] See Article 49 of the Charter of the United Nations; on the special difficulties of Zambia and other African States, see Doxey, *loc. cit.* in note 18, ch. 9, and, for corresponding experiences in the League of Nations, above, p. 32.

[27] *The Economist*, 21 June 1969, p. 16. On the participation of British firms in the Cabora project in Mozambique, see H. C. Deb., Vol. 746, col. 924 *et seq.* (15 December 1969).

[28] *The Economist*, 21 June 1969, p. 16.

[29] *Ibid.*, p. 33.

[30] Res. 317—IV (2 December 1949). See, further, H. Bülck, *Frauenhandel* H.-J. Schlochauer (ed.), *Wörterbuch des Voelkerrechts*, Vol. I (1960) p. 560.

[31] See, further, J. Gutteridge, 'Supplementary Slavery Convention, 1956', 6 *I.C.L.Q.* (1957), p. 449, and C. W. W. Greenidge, *Slavery* (1958), p. 201. By 1 June 1969, 104 States were parties to the I.L.O. Convention No. 29 on Forced Labour (18 June 1930) and 84 States were parties to I.L.O. Convention No. 105 on the Abolition of Forced Labour (25 June 1957). See, further, International Labour Office, *Report of the Ad Hoc Committee on Forced Labour* (1953), and H. Bülck, *Die Zwangsarbeit in Friedensvoelkerrecht* (1953), pp. 139 *et seq.* See also C. N. Jenks, *Human Rights and International Labour Standards* (1960), pp. 39–40, and L. C. Green, 'Human rights in public international law' in L. M. Singhvi (ed.), *Horizons of Freedom* (1969), pp. 93-4.

[32] See, further, J. G. Starke, *Studies in International Law* (1965), p. 44 *et seq.*

[33] Articles 13–22, Cmnd. 584 (1958).

[34] See Article 3 of the 1958 Convention on the High Seas, *supra*, n. 33; the 1965 Convention, 4. I.L.M. (1965), p. 957, or below, Appendix 4, and, further, J. H. E. Fried, 'The 1965 Convention on Transit Trade of land-locked States', 6 *Indian J.I.L.* (1966), p. 9 *et seq.* By 31 December 1968, seventeen States had ratified, or acceded to, the Convention (U.N. Publ. E 69, V. 5, 188). The most far-reaching of the escape clauses was inserted in the draft at the 1965 Diplomatic Conference: 'Nothing in this Convention shall prevent any contracting State from taking any action necessary for the protection of its essential security interests' (Article 11(4), 4 I.L.M. (1965), p. 965).

[35] M. O. Hudson, *International Legislation*, Vol. 1, p. 625. For the status of the Convention and Statute by 31 December 1968, see U.N. Publ. E 69 V. 5, 390. For instance, by 31 December 1968 India was a party to the 1921 Convention, but not to that of 1965. For the bilateral Treaty of Trade and Transit between India and Nepal—the latter is a party to the 1965 Convention—see 1 *Indian J.I.L.* (1961), p. 526.

[36] See, for instance, the Convention of 17 June 1960 (Cmnd. 2812, 1965).

[37] 17 June 1960 (Cmnd. 2956, 1966).

[38] Cmnd. 1535, 1961.

[39] See, for instance, Ph. Jessup and H. J. Taubenfeld, *Controls for Outer Space and the Antarctic Analogy* (1959), and below, p. 62.

[40] Article I (*loc. cit*, above, note 38, p. 2) and Article V (1) (*ibid.*, p. 3).

[41] Article IV(1)(f) (*ibid.*, p. 5).

[42] See Articles VII (*ibid.*, p. 3), VIII (*ibid.*, p. 4), IX (*ibid.*, pp. 4–5), XII (*ibid.*, p. 6) and XIII (*ibid.*, p. 6).

[43] Article XII(2)(a) (*ibid.*, p. 6).

[44] Article XII(1)(b) and (2)(c) (*ibid.*, p. 6).

[45] See, further, J. Hanessian, 'The Antarctic Treaty, 1959', 9 *I.C.L.Q.* (1960), p. 436 *et seq.*

[46] Article XIII(1), *loc. cit.* above, note 38, p. 6.

[47] Para. 4 of the Preamble of the 1961 Convention (Cmnd. 1368, 1961), and para. 5 of the Preamble of the 1963 Convention (Cmnd. 2113, 1963 or below, Appendix 3). See, further, P. Cahier and L. T. Lee, *Vienna Conventions on Diplomatic and Consular Relations*, No. 571 *International Conciliation* (1969).

[48] Article IV (Cmnd. 2245, 1964). See, further, E. Schwelb, 'The nuclear test-ban treaty and international law', 58 *A.J.I.L.* (1964), at p. 660.

[49] *I.L.M.* 811 (1968). See further, O. Kimminich, *Voelkerrecht im Atomzeitalter. Der Atomsperrvertrag und seine Folgen* (1969) and E. B. Firmag, 'The treaty on the non-proliferation of nuclear weapons', 63 *A.J.I.L.* (1969), pp. 711 *et seq.*

[50] Cmnd. 3519 (1968). See, further, J. E. S. Fawcett, *International Law and the Uses of Outer Space* (1968), p. 57 *et seq.*, and Bin Cheng, 'Le Traité de 1967 sur l'espace', 95 *J. Droit international* (1968), pp. 532 *et seq.*

[51] Article 28, Gen. Ass. Res. 217—II (10 December 1948).

[52] On the implementation of the 'International Labour Code' (latest I.L.O. edition, 1952), see, for instance, E. A. Landy, *The Effectiveness of International Supervision* (1966), appendices I and II, and the latest *Chart of Ratification of International Labour Conventions*, published by the International Labour Office, and, on other relevant developments, R. N. Gardner and M. F. Millikan (eds.): 'The global partnership: international agencies and economic development', 22 *International Organization*, No. 1 (1968—special issue).

[53] Cmnd. 3220, 1967; or below, Appendix 5.

See further, E. Schwelb, 'Civil and political rights: the international measures of implementation', 62 *A.J.I.L.* (1968), pp. 827 et seq., and B. A. Wortley, 'Some observations on claims for violations by a State of the human rights of a citizen', 7 *Rivista di Diritto Europeo* (1968), p. 103 *et seq.*

Chapter V

THE OUTLOOK

In this tentative survey of the problem of an international economic order, an attempt has been made to assess the position in unorganised international society and organised international society in the eras of the League of Nations and United Nations.

The most promising evidence available has been selected from the abundance of the relevant material. In its evaluation no preconceived tests were applied. What appeared to matter was to arrive at an assessment which, by the standards of common sense, would almost suggest itself.

It may be advisable, at this point, to recapitulate the criteria applied in the previous lectures to test the eligibility of particular rules as constituent parts of an international economic order:

1. Rules have been examined from the point of view of whether they form part of actual international law or are merely postulates of international morality.

2. Multilateral treaties have been explored from various angles: their duration, the exclusion of reservations, the possibility of renunciation, exception clauses, escape clauses, and the verifiable character of assertions of contingencies mentioned in such clauses.

3. The number and significance of parties to relevant instruments has been taken into account.

4. The continuity of the work carried over from earlier and, perhaps, more modest efforts in earlier phases of the evolution of international society has played its part in the assessment of more extravagant claims made in more recent times.

So long as the tests applied are formulated articulately, anybody is free to accept, reject or modify, as he sees fit, any of these tests or, in applying them to the same or other material, reach different conclusions.

If, as is assumed in these lectures, the primacy of politics over

67

economics applies as much to international society as to national communities in a power-ridden world, one conclusion appears inescapable. It is that no international legal order in the economic field can be stronger than the political order which conditions it. If this is merely an international quasi-order, its subordinate international economic order necessarily belongs to the same category.

On an empirical basis, this statement has been confirmed every time an inter-war period changed into a major war, and never was this more true than in an age of world wars. In each of the two world wars, the economic pre-war order rapidly broke down and was replaced by *ad hoc* wartime economic orders, controlled by the major belligerents.

Even if this decisive aspect of the matter could be ignored, the rules examined in these lectures on the universalist level of the United Nations are too vague, too few and far between, too insignificant and too little verifiable by organs with commensurate jurisdiction —let alone judicial or quasi-judicial detachment—to permit of their classification as a legal world order in economic affairs.

Yet this is not the whole story. This verdict applies only on the universalist level of the United Nations. Perforce, any of the partial orders or quasi-orders falling short of such near-universality have been left out of account. Yet all of them depend, directly or indirectly, on the global system of power politics in disguise, within which all international activities in contemporary world society have to be conducted. Thus they too are inevitably engulfed in this nexus.

So long as this system lasts, it offers scope for and, owing to its own contradictions, fosters international co-operation inside narrower groupings. These may be universalist in intent but, like most of the relevant Specialised Agencies of the United Nations, fall even shorter of universality than the United Nations itself, or they may be of an openly sectional character.

Closer examination of the legal regimes evolved inside these organisations, which is beyond the scope of these lectures, suggests a simple working hypothesis: the more sectional the character of such an institution is, the higher are likely to be the degree of international integration attained and the yield of legally binding rules which, if they were universally applicable, might more properly be termed rules of an economic world order. What they have achieved is the measure of what, so far, has proved unattainable on a universal scale. The conclusion that, so far, no economic world order has emerged could also be expressed in terms more acceptable to those with a teleological bent of mind. If this were desirable, the formulation chosen in Sir Robert Jackson's revealing *Study of the Capacity of the United Nations Development System* could hardly be bettered: 'The United Nations system has taken its first groping steps along the road to world order.'[1] It would be difficult to miss the implied argument *a contrario*.

Whichever version is preferred, the finding has prophylactic, positive and constructive messages:

1. The categories of economic order offered should enable others to evaluate more readily claims advanced on behalf of particular systems to be recognised as world orders rather than classified as mere pseudo-orders or as partial orders with universalist aspirations.

2. If, as is suggested, customary international economic law on a global level lacks any rules of *jus cogens*, the character of these rules as *jus dispositivum* is re-affirmed.

Similarly, the multilateral treaties examined fail to amount to consensual *jus cogens*. Yet, if suitably strengthened by the addition of further parties, stiffened in their peremptory character and augmented by other treaties of economic import, these treaties might well form the nucleus of an economic world order yet to be created.

3. The potential significance of this treaty material suggests the advisability of allocating to it a prominent place in the systematic study of international economic law. A suitable niche for these treaties might be found under the heading which provides their common denominator: the problem of an economic world order.

NOTE

[1] United Nations (Geneva, 1969—DP/5), p. 6.

Appendix 1

RELEVANT ARTICLES OF THE
COVENANT OF THE LEAGUE OF NATIONS

ARTICLE 8 (*Reduction of Armaments*)

1. The Members of the League recognise that the maintenance of peace requires the reduction of national armaments to the lowest point consistent with national safety and the enforcement by common action of international obligations.

2. The Council, taking account of the geographical situation and circumstances of each State, shall formulate plans for such reduction for the consideration and action of the several Governments.

3. Such plans shall be subject to re-consideration and revision at least every ten years.

4. After these plans shall have been adopted by the several Governments, the limits of armaments therein fixed shall not be exceeded without the concurrence of the Council.

5. The Members of the League agree that the manufacture by private enterprise of munitions and implements of war is open to grave objections. The Council shall advise how the evil effects attendant upon such manufacture can be prevented, due regard being had to the necessities of those Members of the League which are not able to manufacture the munitions and implements of war necessary for their safety.

6. The Members of the League undertake to interchange full and frank information as to the scale of their armaments, their military, naval and air programmes and the condition of such of their industries as are adaptable to war-like purposes.

ARTICLE 11 (*Action in case of War or Danger of War*)

1. Any war or threat of war, whether immediately affecting any of the Members of the League or not, is hereby declared a matter of concern to the whole League, and the League shall take any action that may be deemed wise and effectual to safeguard the peace of nations. In case any such emergency should arise the Secretary-General shall on the request of any Member of the League forthwith summon a meeting of the Council.

2. It is also declared to be the friendly right of each Member of the League to bring to the attention of the Assembly or of the Council any circumstance whatever affecting international relations which threatens to disturb international peace or the good understanding between nations upon which peace depends.

ARTICLE 12 (*Disputes to be Submitted to Arbitration or Inquiry*)

1. The Members of the League agree that, if there should arise between them any dispute likely to lead to a rupture, they will submit the matter

70

either to arbitration or judicial settlement or to inquiry by the Council and they agree in no case to resort to war until three months after the award by the arbitrators or the judicial decision, or the report by the Council.

2. In any case under this Article, the award of the arbitrators or the judicial decision shall be made within a reasonable time, and the report of the Council shall be made within six months after the submission of the dispute.

ARTICLE 13 (*Arbitration of Disputes*)

1. The Members of the League agree that, whenever any dispute shall arise between them which they recognise to be suitable for submission to arbitration or judicial settlement, and which cannot be satisfactorily settled by diplomacy, they will submit the whole subject-matter to arbitration or judicial settlement.

2. Disputes as to the interpretation of a treaty, as to any question of international law, as to the existence of any fact which, if established, would constitute a breach of any international obligation, or as to the extent and nature of the reparation to be made for any such breach, are declared to be among those which are generally suitable for submission to arbitration or judicial settlement.

3. For the consideration of any such dispute, the court to which the case is referred shall be the Permanent Court of International Justice, established in accordance with Article 14, or any tribunal agreed on by the parties to the dispute or stipulated in any convention existing between them.

4. The Members of the League agree that they will carry out in full good faith any award or decision that may be rendered, and that they will not resort to war against any Member of the League that complies therewith. In the event of any failure to carry out such an award or decision, the Council shall propose what steps should be taken to give effect thereto.

ARTICLE 14 (*Permanent Court of International Justice*)

The Council shall formulate and submit to the Members of the League for adoption plans for the establishment of a Permanent Court of International Justice. The Court shall be competent to hear and determine any dispute of an international character which the parties thereto submit to it. The Court may also give an advisory opinion upon any dispute or question referred to it by the Council or by the Assembly.

ARTICLE 15 (*Disputes Not Submitted to Arbitration*)

1. If there should arise between Members of the League any dispute likely to lead to a rupture, which is not submitted to arbitration or judicial settlement in accordance with Article 13, the Members of the League agree that they will submit the matter to the Council. Any party to the dispute may effect such submission by giving notice of the existence of the dispute to the Secretary-General, who will make all necessary arrangements for a full investigation and consideration thereof.

2. For this purpose the parties to the dispute will communicate to the Secretary-General, as promptly as possible, statements of their case, with

all the relevant facts and papers, and the Council may forthwith direct the publication thereof.

3. The Council shall endeavour to effect a settlement of the dispute, and if such efforts are successful, a statement shall be made public giving such facts and explanations regarding the dispute and the terms of settlement thereof as the Council may deem appropriate.

4. If the dispute is not thus settled, the Council either unanimously or by a majority vote shall make and publish a report containing a statement of the facts of the dispute and the recommendations which are deemed just and proper in regard thereto.

5. Any Member of the League represented on the Council may make public a statement of the facts of the dispute and of its conclusions regarding the same.

6. If a report by the Council is unanimously agreed to by the members thereof other than the Representatives of one or more of the parties to the dispute, the Members of the League agree that they will not go to war with any party to the dispute which complies with the recommendations of the report.

7. If the Council fails to reach a report which is unanimously agreed to by the members thereof, other than the Representatives of one or more of the parties to the dispute, the Members of the League reserve to themselves the right to take such action as they shall consider necessary for the maintenance of right and justice.

8. If the dispute between the parties is claimed by one of them and is found by the Council to arise out of a matter which by international law is solely within the domestic jurisdiction of that party, the Council shall so report, and shall make no recommendation as to its settlement.

9. The Council may in any case under this Article refer the dispute to the Assembly. The dispute shall be so referred at the request of either party to the dispute, provided that such request be made within fourteen days after the submission of the dispute to the Council.

10. In any case referred to the Assembly, all the provisions of this Article and of Article 12 relating to the action and powers of the Council shall apply to the action and powers of the Assembly, provided that a report made by the Assembly, if concurred in by the Representatives of those Members of the League represented on the Council and of a majority of the other Members of the League, exclusive in each case of the representatives of the parties to the dispute, shall have the same force as a report by the Council concurred in by all the members thereof other than the Representatives of one or more of the parties to the dispute.

ARTICLE 16 (*League Sanctions*)

1. Should any Member of the League resort to war in disregard of its covenants under Articles 12, 13 or 15, it shall *ipso facto* be deemed to have committed an act of war against all other Members of the League, which hereby undertake immediately to subject it to the severance of all trade or financial relations, the prohibition of all intercourse between their nationals and the nationals of the covenant-breaking State, and the prevention of all financial, commercial or personal intercourse between

the nationals of the covenant-breaking State and the nationals of any other State, whether a Member of the League or not.

2. It shall be the duty of the Council in such case to recommend to the several Governments concerned what effective military, naval or air force the Members of the League shall severally contribute to the armed forces to be used to protect the covenants of the League.

3. The Members of the League agree, further, that they will mutually support one another in the financial and economic measures which are taken under this Article, in order to minimise the loss and inconvenience resulting from the above measures, and that they will mutually support one another in resisting any special measures aimed at one of their number by the covenant-breaking State, and that they will take the necessary steps to afford passage through their territory to the forces of any of the Members of the League which are co-operating to protect the covenants of the League.

4. Any Member of the League which has violated any covenant of the League may be declared to be no longer a Member of the League by a vote of the Council concurred in by the Representatives of all the other Members of the League represented thereon.

ARTICLE 17 (*Disputes with Non-Members*)

1. In the event of a dispute between a Member of the League and a State which is not a Member of the League, or between States not Members of the League, the State or States not Members of the League shall be invited to accept the obligations of membership in the League for the purposes of such dispute, upon such conditions as the Council may deem just. If such invitation is accepted, the provisions of Articles 12 to 16 inclusive shall be applied with such modifications as may be deemed necessary by the Council.

2. Upon such invitation being given the Council shall immediately institute an inquiry into the circumstances of the dispute and recommend such action as may seem best and most effectual in the circumstances.

3. If a State so invited shall refuse to accept the obligations of membership in the League for the purposes of such dispute, and shall resort to war against a Member of the League, the provisions of Article 16 shall be applicable as against the State taking such action.

4. If both parties to the dispute when so invited refuse to accept the obligations of membership in the League for the purposes of such dispute, the Council may take such measures and make such recommendations as will prevent hostilities and will result in the settlement of the dispute.

ARTICLE 22 (*League Mandates*)

1. To those colonies and territories which as a consequence of the late war have ceased to be under the sovereignty of the States which formerly governed them and which are inhabited by peoples not yet able to stand by themselves under the strenuous conditions of the modern world, there should be applied the principle that the well-being and development of such peoples form a sacred trust of civilisation and that securities for the performance of this trust should be embodied in this Covenant.

2. The best method of giving practical effect to this principle is that the tutelage of such people should be entrusted to advanced nations who by reason of their resources, their experience, or their geographical position can best undertake this responsibility, and who are willing to accept it, and that this tutelage should be exercised by them as Mandatories on behalf of the League.

3. The character of the mandate must differ according to the stage of the development of the people, the geographical situation of the territory, its economic conditions and other similar circumstances.

4. Certain communities formerly belonging to the Turkish Empire have reached a stage of development where their existence as independent nations can be provisionally recognised subject to the rendering of administrative advice and assistance by a Mandatory until such times as they are able to stand alone. The wishes of these communities must be a principal consideration in the selection of the Mandatory.

5. Other peoples, especially those of Central Africa, are at such a stage that the Mandatory must be responsible for the administration of the territory under conditions which will guarantee freedom of conscience and religion, subject only to the maintenance of public order and morals, the prohibition of abuses such as the slave trade, the arms traffic and the liquor traffic, and the prevention of the establishment of fortifications or military and naval bases and of military training of the natives for other than police purposes and the defence of territory, and will also secure equal opportunities for the trade and commerce of other Members of the League.

6. There are territories, such as South-West Africa and certain of the South Pacific Islands, which, owing to the sparseness of their population, or their small size, or their remoteness from the centres of civilisation, or their geographical contiguity to the territory of the Mandatory, and other circumstances, can be best administered under the laws of the Mandatory, as integral portions of its territory, subject to the safeguards above-mentioned in the interests of the indigenous population.

7. In every case of mandate, the Mandatory shall render to the Council an annual report in reference to the territory committed to its charge.

8. The degree of authority, control, or administration to be exercised by the Mandatory shall, if not previously agreed upon by the Members of the League, be explicitly defined in each case by the Council.

9. A permanent Commission shall be constituted to receive and examine the annual reports of the Mandatories and to advise the Council on all matters relating to the observance of the mandates.

ARTICLE 23 (*Economic and Social Activities*)

Subject to and in accordance with the provisions of international conventions existing or hereafter to be agreed upon, the Members of the League:

(*a*) will endeavour to secure and maintain fair and humane conditions of labour for men, women and children, both in their own countries and in all countries to which their commercial and industrial relations extend, and for that purpose will establish and maintain the necessary international organisations;

(b) undertake to secure just treatment of the native inhabitants of territories under their control;

(c) will entrust the League with the general supervision over the execution of agreements with regard to the traffic in women and children, and the traffic in opium and other dangerous drugs;

(d) will entrust the League with the general supervision of the trade in arms and ammunition with the countries in which the control of this traffic is necessary in the common interest;

(e) will make provision to secure and maintain freedom of communications and of transit and equitable treatment for the commerce of all Members of the League. In this connection, the special necessities of the regions devastated during the war of 1914–1918 shall be borne in mind;

(f) will endeavour to take steps in matters of international concern for the prevention and control of disease.

Appendix 2

CHAPTERS IX AND X
OF THE UNITED NATIONS CHARTER

CHAPTER IX

INTERNATIONAL ECONOMIC AND SOCIAL CO-OPERATION

Article 55

With a view to the creation of conditions of stability and well-being which are necessary for peaceful and friendly relations among nations based on respect for the principle of equal rights and self-determination of peoples, the United Nations shall promote:

(*a*) Higher standards of living, full employment, and conditions of economic and social progress and development;

(*b*) solutions of international economic, social, health and related problems; and international cultural and educational co-operation; and

(*c*) universal respect for, and observance of, human rights and fundamental freedoms for all without distinction as to race, sex, language or religion.

Article 56

All Members pledge themselves to take joint and separate action in co-operation with the Organisation for the achievement of the purposes set forth in Article 55.

Article 57

1. The various specialised agencies, established by inter-governmental agreement and having wide international responsibilities, as defined in their basic instruments, in economic, social, cultural, educational, health and related fields, shall be brought into relationship with the United Nations in accordance with the provisions of Article 63.

2. Such agencies thus brought into relationship with the United Nations are hereinafter referred to as specialised agencies.

Article 58

The Organisation shall make recommendations for the co-ordination of the policies and activities of the specialised agencies.

Article 59

The Organisation shall, where appropriate, initiate negotiations among the states concerned for the creation of any new specialised agencies required for the accomplishment of the purposes set forth in Article 55.

Article 60

Responsibility for the discharge of the functions of the Organisation set forth in this Chapter shall be vested in the General Assembly and, under the authority of the General Assembly, in the Economic and Social Council, which shall have for this purpose the powers set forth in Chapter X.

CHAPTER X

THE ECONOMIC AND SOCIAL COUNCIL COMPOSITION

Article 61

1. The Economic and Social Council shall consist of 27 Members of the United Nations elected by the General Assembly.

2. Subject to the provisions of paragraph 3, nine members of the Economic and Social Council shall be elected each year for a term of three years. A retiring member shall be eligible for immediate re-election.

3. At the first election after the increase in the membership of the Economic and Social Council from eighteen to twenty-seven members, in addition to the members elected in place of the six members whose term of office expires at the end of that year, nine additional members shall be elected. Of these nine additional members, the term of office of three members so elected shall expire at the end of one year, and of three other members at the end of two years, in accordance with arrangements made by the General Assembly.

4. Each member of the Economic and Social Council shall have one representative.

FUNCTIONS AND POWERS

Article 62

1. The Economic and Social Council may make or initiate studies and reports with respect to international, economic, social, cultural, educational, health and related matters and may make recommendations with respect to any such matters to the General Assembly, to the Members of the United Nations, and to the specialised agencies concerned.

2. It may make recommendations for the purpose of promoting respect for, and observance of, human rights and fundamental freedoms for all.

3. It may prepare draft conventions for submission to the General Assembly, with respect to matters falling within its competence.

4. It may call, in accordance with the rules prescribed by the United Nations, international conferences on matters falling within its competence.

Article 63

1. The Economic and Social Council may enter into agreements with any of the agencies referred to in Article 57, defining the terms on which the agency concerned shall be brought into relationship with the United

Nations. Such agreements shall be subject to approval by the General Assembly.

2. It may co-ordinate the activities of the specialised agencies through consultation with and recommendations to such agencies and through recommendations to the General Assembly and to the Members of the United Nations.

Article 64

1. The Economic and Social Council may take appropriate steps to obtain regular reports from the specialised agencies. It may make arrangements with the Members of the United Nations and with the specialised agencies to obtain reports on the steps taken to give effect to its own recommendations and to recommendations on matters falling within its competence made by the General Assembly.

2. It may communicate its observations on these reports to the General Assembly.

Article 65

The Economic and Social Council may furnish information to the Security Council and shall assist the Security Council upon its request.

Article 66

1. The Economic and Social Council shall perform such functions as fall within its competence in connection with the carrying out of the recommendations of the General Assembly.

2. It may, with the approval of the General Assembly, perform services at the request of Members of the United Nations and at the request of specialised agencies.

3. It shall perform such other functions as are specified elsewhere in the present Charter or as may be assigned to it by the General Assembly.

VOTING

Article 67

1. Each member of the Economic and Social Council shall have one vote.

2. Decisions of the Economic and Social Council shall be made by a majority of the members present and voting.

PROCEDURE

Article 68

The Economic and Social Council shall set up commissions in economic and social fields and for the promotion of human rights, and such other commissions as may be required for the performance of its functions.

Article 69

The Economic and Social Council shall invite any Member of the United Nations to participate, without vote, in its deliberations on any matter of particular concern to that Member.

APPENDIX 2

Article 70

The Economic and Social Council may make arrangements for representatives of the specialised agencies to participate, without vote, in its deliberations and in those of the commissions established by it, and for its representatives to participate in the deliberations of the specialised agencies.

Article 71

The Economic and Social Council may make suitable arrangements for consultation with non-governmental organisations which are concerned with matters within its competence.

Such arrangements may be made with international organisations and, where appropriate, with national organisations after consultation with the Member of the United Nations concerned.

Article 72

1. The Economic and Social Council shall adopt its own rules of procedure, including the method of selecting its President.

2. The Economic and Social Council shall meet as required in accordance with its rules, which shall include provision for the convening of meetings on request of a majority of its members.

Appendix 3

VIENNA CONVENTION ON CONSULAR RELATIONS

24 April 1963

THE STATES PARTIES TO THE PRESENT CONVENTION,

RECALLING that consular relations have been established between peoples since ancient times,

HAVING IN MIND the Purposes and Principles of the Charter of the United Nations concerning the sovereign equality of States, the maintenance of international peace and security, and the promotion of friendly relations among nations,

CONSIDERING that the United Nations Conference on Diplomatic Intercourse and Immunities adopted the Vienna Convention on Diplomatic Relations which was opened for signature on 18 April 1961,

BELIEVING that an international convention on consular relations, privileges and immunities would also contribute to the development of friendly relations among nations, irrespective of their differing constitutional and social systems,

REALIZING that the purpose of such privileges and immunities is not to benefit individuals but to ensure the efficient performance of functions by consular posts on behalf of their respective States,

AFFIRMING that the rules of customary international law continue to govern matters not expressly regulated by the provisions of the present Convention,

HAVE AGREED as follows:

ARTICLE 1

Definitions

1. For the purposes of the present Convention, the following expressions shall have the meanings hereunder assigned to them:

   (*a*) 'consular post' means any consulate-general, consulate, vice-consulate or consular agency;

   (*b*) 'consular district' means the area assigned to a consular post for the exercise of consular functions;

   (*c*) 'head of consular post' means the person charged with the duty of acting in that capacity;

   (*d*) 'consular officer' means any person, including the head of a consular post, entrusted in that capacity with the exercise of consular functions;

80

(e) 'consular employee' means any person employed in the administrative or technical service of a consular post;

(f) 'member of the service staff' means any person employed in the domestic service of a consular post;

(g) 'members of the consular post' means consular officers, consular employees and members of the service staff;

(h) 'members of the consular staff' means consular officers, other than the head of a consular post, consular employees and members of the service staff;

(i) 'member of the private staff' means a person who is employed exclusively in the private service of a member of the consular post;

(j) 'consular premises' means the buildings or parts of buildings and the land ancillary thereto, irrespective of ownership, used exclusively for the purposes of the consular post;

(k) 'consular archives' includes all the papers, documents, correspondence, books, films, tapes and registers of the consular post, together with the ciphers and codes, the card-indexes and any article of furniture intended for their protection or safekeeping.

2. Consular officers are of two categories, namely career consular officers and honorary consular officers. The provisions of Chapter II of the present Convention apply to consular posts headed by career consular officers; the provisions of Chapter III govern consular posts headed by honorary consular officers.

3. The particular status of members of the consular posts who are nationals or permanent residents of the receiving State is governed by Article 71 of the present Convention.

CHAPTER I.—CONSULAR RELATIONS IN GENERAL

SECTION I.—ESTABLISHMENT AND CONDUCT OF CONSULAR RELATIONS

ARTICLE 2

Establishment of consular relations

1. The establishment of consular relations between States takes place by mutual consent.

2. The consent given to the establishment of diplomatic relations between two States implies, unless otherwise stated, consent to the establishment of consular relations.

3. The severance of diplomatic relations shall not *ipso facto* involve the severance of consular relations.

ARTICLE 3

Exercise of consular functions

Consular functions are exercised by consular posts. They are also exercised by diplomatic missions in accordance with the provisions of the present Convention.

ARTICLE 4

Establishment of a consular post

1. A consular post may be established in the territory of the receiving State only with that State's consent.

2. The seat of the consular post, its classification and the consular district shall be established by the sending State and shall be subject to the approval of the receiving State.

3. Subsequent changes in the seat of the consular post, its classification or the consular district may be made by the sending State only with the consent of the receiving State.

4. The consent of the receiving State shall also be required if a consulate-general or a consulate desires to open a vice-consulate or a consular agency in a locality other than that in which it is itself established.

5. The prior express consent of the receiving State shall also be required for the opening of an office forming part of an existing consular post elsewhere than at the seat thereof.

ARTICLE 5

Consular functions

Consular functions consist in:

(a) protecting in the receiving State the interests of the sending State and of its nationals, both individuals and bodies corporate, within the limits permitted by international law;

(b) furthering the development of commercial, economic, cultural and scientific relations between the sending State and the receiving State and otherwise promoting friendly relations between them in accordance with the provisions of the present Convention;

(c) ascertaining by all lawful means conditions and developments in the commercial, economic, cultural and scientific life of the receiving State, reporting thereon to the Government of the sending State and giving information to persons interested;

(d) issuing passports and travel documents to nationals of the sending State, and visas or appropriate documents to persons wishing to travel to the sending State;

(e) helping and assisting nationals, both individuals and bodies corporate, of the sending State;

(f) acting as notary and civil registrar and in capacities of a similar kind, and performing certain functions of an administrative nature, provided that there is nothing contrary thereto in the laws and regulations of the receiving State;

(g) safeguarding the interests of nationals, both individuals and bodies corporate, of the sending State in cases of succession *mortis causa* in the territory of the receiving State, in accordance with the laws and regulations of the receiving State;

(h) safeguarding, within the limits imposed by the laws and regulations of the receiving State, the interests of minors and other persons lacking full capacity who are nationals of the sending State, par-

82

ticularly where any guardianship or trusteeship is required with respect to such persons;

(*i*) subject to the practices and procedures obtaining in the receiving State, representing or arranging appropriate representation for nationals of the sending State before the tribunals and other authorities of the receiving State, for the purpose of obtaining, in accordance with the laws and regulations of the receiving State, provisional measures for the preservation of the rights and interests of these nationals, where, because of absence or any other reason, such nationals are unable at the proper time to assume the defence of their rights and interests;

(*j*) transmitting judicial and extra-judicial documents or executing letters rogatory or commissions to take evidence for the courts of the sending State in accordance with international agreements in force or, in the absence of such international agreements, in any other manner compatible with the laws and regulations of the receiving State;

(*k*) exercising rights of supervision and inspection provided for in the laws and regulations of the sending State in respect of vessels having the nationality of the sending State, and of aircraft registered in that State, and in respect of their crews;

(*l*) extending assistance to vessels and aircraft mentioned in subparagraph (*k*) of this Article, and to their crews, taking statements regarding the voyage of a vessel, examining and stamping the ship's papers, and, without prejudice to the powers of the authorities of the receiving State, conducting investigations into any incidents which occurred during the voyage, and settling disputes of any kind between the master, the officers and the seamen in so far as this may be authorized by the laws and regulations of the sending State;

(*m*) performing any other functions entrusted to a consular post by the sending State which are not prohibited by the laws and regulations of the receiving State or to which no objection is taken by the receiving State or which are referred to in the international agreements in force between the sending State and the receiving State.

ARTICLE 6

Exercise of consular functions outside the consular district

A consular officer may, in special circumstances, with the consent of the receiving State, exercise his functions outside his consular district.

ARTICLE 7

Exercise of consular functions in a third State

The sending State may, after notifying the States concerned, entrust a consular post established in a particular State with the exercise of consular functions in another State, unless there is express objection by one of the States concerned.

ARTICLE 8

Exercise of consular functions on behalf of a third State

Upon appropriate notification to the receiving State, a consular post of the sending State may, unless the receiving State objects, exercise consular functions in the receiving State on behalf of a third State.

ARTICLE 9

Classes of heads of consular posts

1. Heads of consular posts are divided into four classes, namely:
(a) consuls-general;
(b) consuls;
(c) vice-consuls;
(d) consular agents.
2. Paragraph 1 of this Article in no way restricts the right of any of the Contracting Parties to fix the designation of consular officers other than the heads of consular posts.

ARTICLE 10

Appointment and admission of heads of consular posts

1. Heads of consular posts are appointed by the sending State and are admitted to the exercise of their functions by the receiving State.
2. Subject to the provisions of the present Convention, the formalities for the appointment and for the admission of the head of a consular post are determined by the laws, regulations and usages of the sending State and of the receiving State respectively.

ARTICLE 11

The consular commission or notification of appointment

1. The head of a consular post shall be provided by the sending State with a document, in the form of a commission or similar instrument, made out for each appointment certifying his capacity and showing, as a general rule, his full name, his category and class, the consular district and the seat of the consular post.
2. The sending State shall transmit the commission or similar instrument through the diplomatic or other appropriate channel to the Government of the State in whose territory the head of a consular post is to exercise his functions.
3. If the receiving State agrees, the sending State may, instead of a commission or similar instrument, send to the receiving State a notification containing the particulars required by paragraph 1 of this Article.

ARTICLE 12

The exequatur

1. The head of a consular post is admitted to the exercise of his functions by an authorization from the receiving State termed an *exequatur*, whatever the form of this authorization.

84

2. A State which refuses to grant an *exequatur* is not obliged to give to the sending State reasons for such refusal.

3. Subject to the provisions of Articles 13 and 15, the head of a consular post shall not enter upon his duties until he has received an *exequatur*.

ARTICLE 13

Provisional admission of heads of consular posts

Pending the delivery of the *exequatur*, the head of a consular post may be admitted on a provisional basis to the exercise of his functions. In that case, the provisions of the present Convention shall apply.

ARTICLE 14

Notification to the authorities of the consular district

As soon as the head of a consular post is admitted even provisionally to the exercise of his functions, the receiving State shall immediately notify the competent authorities of the consular district. It shall also ensure that the necessary measures are taken to enable the head of a consular post to carry out the duties of his office and to have the benefit of the provisions of the present Convention.

ARTICLE 15

Temporary exercise of the functions of the head of a consular post

1. If the head of a consular post is unable to carry out his functions or the position of head of consular post is vacant, an acting head of post may act provisionally as head of the consular post.

2. The full name of the acting head of post shall be notified either by the diplomatic mission of the sending State or, if that State has no such mission in the receiving State, by the head of the consular post, or, if he is unable to do so, by a competent authority of the sending State, to the Ministry for Foreign Affairs of the receiving State or to the authority designated by that Ministry. As a general rule, this notification shall be given in advance. The receiving State may make the admission as acting head of post of a person who is neither a diplomatic agent nor a consular officer of the sending State in the receiving State conditional on its consent.

3. The competent authorities of the receiving State shall afford assistance and protection to the acting head of post. While he is in charge of the post, the provisions of the present Convention shall apply to him on the same basis as to the head of the consular post concerned. The receiving State shall not, however, be obliged to grant to an acting head of post any facility, privilege or immunity which the head of the consular post enjoys only subject to conditions not fulfilled by the acting head of post.

4. When, in the circumstances referred to in paragraph 1 of this Article, a member of the diplomatic staff of the diplomatic mission of the sending State in the receiving State is designated by the sending State as an acting head of post, he shall, if the receiving State does not object thereto, continue to enjoy diplomatic privileges and immunities.

ARTICLE 16

Precedence as between heads of consular posts

1. Heads of consular posts shall rank in each class according to the date of the grant of the *exequatur*.

2. If, however, the head of a consular post before obtaining the *exequatur* is admitted to the exercise of his functions provisionally, his precedence shall be determined according to the date of the provisional admission; this precedence shall be maintained after the granting of the *exequatur*.

3. The order of precedence as between two or more heads of consular posts who obtained the *exequatur* or provisional admission on the same date shall be determined according to the dates on which their commissions or similar instruments or the notifications referred to in paragraph 3 of Article 11 were presented to the receiving State.

4. Acting heads of posts shall rank after all heads of consular posts and, as between themselves, they shall rank according to the dates on which they assumed their functions as acting heads of posts as indicated in the notifications given under paragraph 2 of Article 15.

5. Honorary consular officers who are heads of consular posts shall rank in each class after career heads of consular posts, in the order and according to the rules laid down in the foregoing paragraphs.

6. Heads of consular posts shall have precedence over consular officers not having that status.

ARTICLE 17

Performance of diplomatic acts by consular officers

1. In a State where the sending State has no diplomatic mission and is not represented by a diplomatic mission of a third State, a consular officer may, with the consent of the receiving State, and without affecting his consular status, be authorized to perform diplomatic acts. The performance of such acts by a consular officer shall not confer upon him any right to claim diplomatic privileges and immunities.

2. A consular officer may, after notification addressed to the receiving State, act as representative of the sending State to any inter-governmental organization. When so acting, he shall be entitled to enjoy any privileges and immunities accorded to such a representative by customary international law or by international agreements; however, in respect of the performance by him of any consular function, he shall not be entitled to any greater immunity from jurisdiction than that to which a consular officer is entitled under the present Convention.

ARTICLE 18

Appointment of the same person by two or more States as a consular officer

Two or more States may, with the consent of the receiving State, appoint the same person as a consular officer in that State.

86

APPENDIX 3

ARTICLE 19

Appointment of members of consular staff

1. Subject to the provisions of Articles 20, 22 and 23, the sending State may freely appoint the members of the consular staff.

2. The full name, category and class of all consular officers, other than the head of a consular post, shall be notified by the sending State to the receiving State in sufficient time for the receiving State, if it so wishes, to exercise its rights under paragraph 3 of Article 23.

3. The sending State may, if required by its laws and regulations, request the receiving State to grant an *exequatur* to a consular officer other than the head of a consular post.

4. The receiving State may, if required by its laws and regulations, grant an *exequatur* to a consular officer other than the head of a consular post.

ARTICLE 20

Size of the consular staff

In the absence of an express agreement as to the size of the consular staff, the receiving State may require that the size of the staff be kept within limits considered by it to be reasonable and normal, having regard to circumstances and conditions in the consular district and to the needs of the particular consular post.

ARTICLE 21

Precedence as between consular officers of a consular post

The order of precedence as between the consular officers of a consular post and any change thereof shall be notified by the diplomatic mission of the sending State or, if that State has no such mission in the receiving State, by the head of the consular post, to the Ministry for Foreign Affairs of the receiving State or to the authority designated by that Ministry.

ARTICLE 22

Nationality of consular officers

1. Consular officers should, in principle, have the nationality of the sending State.

2. Consular officers may not be appointed from among persons having the nationality of the receiving State except with the express consent of that State which may be withdrawn at any time.

3. The receiving State may reserve the same right with regard to nationals of a third State who are not also nationals of the sending State.

ARTICLE 23

Persons declared non grata

1. The receiving State may at any time notify the sending State that a consular officer is *persona non grata* or that any other member of the

87

consular staff is not acceptable. In that event, the sending State shall, as the case may be, either recall the person concerned or terminate his functions with the consular post.

2. If the sending State refuses or fails within a reasonable time to carry out its obligations under paragraph 1 of this Article, the receiving State may, as the case may be, either withdraw the *exequatur* from the person concerned or cease to consider him as a member of the consular staff.

3. A person appointed as a member of a consular post may be declared unacceptable before arriving in the territory of the receiving State or, if already in the receiving State, before entering on his duties with the consular post. In any such case, the sending State shall withdraw his appointment.

4. In the cases mentioned in paragraphs 1 and 3 of this Article, the receiving State is not obliged to give to the sending State reasons for its decision.

ARTICLE 24

Notification to the receiving State of appointments, arrivals and departures

1. The Ministry for Foreign Affairs of the receiving State or the authority designated by that Ministry shall be notified of:

(a) the appointment of members of a consular post, their arrival after appointment to the consular post, their final departure or the termination of their functions and any other changes affecting their status that may occur in the course of their service with the consular post;

(b) the arrival and final departure of a person belonging to the family of a member of a consular post forming part of his household and, where appropriate, the fact that a person becomes or ceases to be such a member of the family;

(c) the arrival and final departure of members of the private staff and, where appropriate, the termination of their service as such;

(d) the engagement and discharge of persons resident in the receiving State as members of a consular post or as members of the private staff entitled to privileges and immunities.

2. When possible, prior notification of arrival and final departure shall also be given.

SECTION II.—END OF CONSULAR FUNCTIONS

ARTICLE 25

Termination of the functions of a member of a consular post

The functions of a member of a consular post shall come to an end *inter alia:*

(a) on notification by the sending State to the receiving State that his functions have come to an end;

(b) on withdrawal of the *exequatur*;

(c) on notification by the receiving State to the sending State that the receiving State has ceased to consider him as a member of the consular staff.

ARTICLE 26

Departure from the territory of the receiving State

The receiving State shall, even in case of armed conflict, grant to members of the consular post and members of the private staff, other than nationals of the receiving State, and to members of their families forming part of their households irrespective of nationality, the necessary time and facilities to enable them to prepare their departure and to leave at the earliest possible moment after the termination of the functions of the members concerned. In particular, it shall, in the case of need, place at their disposal the necessary means of transport for themselves and their property other than property acquired in the receiving State the export of which is prohibited at the time of departure.

ARTICLE 27

Protection of consular premises and archives and of the interests of the sending State in exceptional circumstances

1. In the event of the severance of consular relations between two States:

(a) the receiving State shall, even in case of armed conflict, respect and protect the consular premises, together with the property of the consular post and the consular archives;

(b) the sending State may entrust the custody of the consular premises, together with the property contained therein and the consular archives, to a third State acceptable to the receiving State;

(c) the sending State may entrust the protection of its interests and those of its nationals to a third State acceptable to the receiving State.

2. In the event of the temporary or permanent closure of a consular post, the provisions of sub-paragraph (a) of paragraph 1 of this Article shall apply. In addition,

(a) if the sending State, although not represented in the receiving State by a diplomatic mission, has another consular post in the territory of that State, that consular post may be entrusted with the custody of the premises of the consular post which has been closed, together with the property contained therein and the consular archives, and, with the consent of the receiving State, with the exercise of consular functions in the district of that consular post; or

(b) if the sending State has no diplomatic mission and no other consular post in the receiving State, the provisions of sub-paragraphs (b) and (c) of paragraph 1 of this Article shall apply.

CHAPTER II.—FACILITIES, PRIVILEGES AND IMMUNITIES RELATING TO CONSULAR POSTS, CAREER CONSULAR OFFICERS AND OTHER MEMBERS OF A CONSULAR POST

SECTION I.—FACILITIES, PRIVILEGES AND IMMUNITIES RELATING TO A CONSULAR POST

ARTICLE 28

Facilities for the work of the consular post

The receiving State shall accord full facilities for the performance of the functions of the consular post.

ARTICLE 29

Use of national flag and coat-of-arms

1. The sending State shall have the right to the use of its national flag and coat-of-arms in the receiving State in accordance with the provisions of this Article.

2. The national flag of the sending State may be flown and its coat-of-arms displayed on the building occupied by the consular post and at the entrance door thereof, on the residence of the head of the consular post and on his means of transport when used on official business.

3. In the exercise of the right accorded by this Article regard shall be had to the laws, regulations and usages of the receiving State.

ARTICLE 30

Accommodation

1. The receiving State shall either facilitate the acquisition on its territory, in accordance with its laws and regulations, by the sending State of premises necessary for its consular post or assist the latter in obtaining accommodation in some other way.

2. It shall also, where necessary, assist the consular post in obtaining suitable accommodation for its members.

ARTICLE 31

Inviolability of the consular premises

1. Consular premises shall be inviolable to the extent provided in this Article.

2. The authorities of the receiving State shall not enter that part of the consular premises which is used exclusively for the purpose of the work of the consular post except with the consent of the head of the consular post or of his designee or of the head of the diplomatic mission of the sending State. The consent of the head of the consular post may, however, be assumed in case of fire or other disaster requiring prompt protective action.

3. Subject to the provisions of paragraph 2 of this Article, the receiving

90

State is under a special duty to take all appropriate steps to protect the consular premises against any intrusion or damage and to prevent any disturbance of the peace of the consular post or impairment of its dignity.

4. The consular premises, their furnishings, the property of the consular post and its means of transport shall be immune from any form of requisition for purposes of national defence or public utility. If expropriation is necessary for such purposes, all possible steps shall be taken to avoid impeding the performance of consular functions, and prompt, adequate and effective compensation shall be paid to the sending State.

ARTICLE 32

Exemption from taxation of consular premises

1. Consular premises and the residence of the career head of consular post of which the sending State or any person acting on its behalf is the owner or lessee shall be exempt from all national, regional or municipal dues and taxes whatsoever, other than such as represent payment for specific services rendered.

2. The exemption from taxation referred to in paragraph 1 of this Article shall not apply to such dues and taxes if, under the law of the receiving State, they are payable by the person who contracted with the sending State or with the person acting on its behalf.

ARTICLE 33

Inviolability of the consular archives and documents

The consular archives and documents shall be inviolable at all times and wherever they may be.

ARTICLE 34

Freedom of movement

Subject to its laws and regulations concerning zones entry into which is prohibited or regulated for reasons of national security, the receiving State shall ensure freedom of movement and travel in its territory to all members of the consular post.

ARTICLE 35

Freedom of communication

1. The receiving State shall permit and protect freedom of communication on the part of the consular post for all official purposes. In communicating with the Government, the diplomatic missions and other consular posts, wherever situated, of the sending State, the consular post may employ all appropriate means, including diplomatic or consular couriers, diplomatic or consular bags and messages in code or cipher. However, the consular post may install and use a wireless transmitter only with the consent of the receiving State.

2. The official correspondence of the consular post shall be inviolable.

91

Official correspondence means all correspondence relating to the consular post and its functions.

3. The consular bag shall be neither opened nor detained. Nevertheless, if the competent authorities of the receiving State have serious reason to believe that the bag contains something other than the correspondence, documents or articles referred to in paragraph 4 of this Article, they may request that the bag be opened in their presence by an authorized representative of the sending State. If this request is refused by the authorities of the sending State, the bag shall be returned to its place of origin.

4. The packages constituting the consular bag shall bear visible external marks of their character and may contain only official correspondence and documents or articles intended exclusively for official use.

5. The consular courier shall be provided with an official document indicating his status and the number of packages constituting the consular bag. Except with the consent of the receiving State he shall be neither a national of the receiving State, nor, unless he is a national of the sending State, a permanent resident of the receiving State. In the performance of his functions he shall be protected by the receiving State. He shall enjoy personal inviolability and shall not be liable to any form of arrest or detention.

6. The sending State, its diplomatic missions and its consular posts may designate consular couriers *ad hoc*. In such cases the provisions of paragraph 5 of this Article shall also apply except that the immunities therein mentioned shall cease to apply when such a courier has delivered to the consignee the consular bag in his charge.

7. A consular bag may be entrusted to the captain of a ship or of a commercial aircraft scheduled to land at an authorized port of entry. He shall be provided with an official document indicating the number of packages constituting the bag, but he shall not be considered to be a consular courier. By arrangement with the appropriate local authorities, the consular post may send one of its members to take possession of the bag directly and freely from the captain of the ship or of the aircraft.

ARTICLE 36

Communication and contact with nationals of the sending State

1. With a view to facilitating the exercise of consular functions relating to nationals of the sending State:

(a) consular officers shall be free to communicate with nationals of the sending State and to have access to them. Nationals of the sending State shall have the same freedom with respect to communication with and access to consular officers of the sending State:

(b) if he so requests, the competent authorities of the receiving State shall, without delay, inform the consular post of the sending State if, within its consular district, a national of that State is arrested or committed to prison or to custody pending trial or is detained in any other manner. Any communication addressed to the consular post by the person arrested, in prison, custody or detention shall also be forwarded by the said authorities without delay. The said authorities shall inform the person concerned without delay of his rights under this sub-paragraph;

(c) consular officers shall have the right to visit a national of the sending State who is in prison, custody or detention, to converse and correspond with him and to arrange for his legal representation. They shall also have the right to visit any national of the sending State who is in prison, custody or detention in their district in pursuance of a judgment. Nevertheless, consular officers shall refrain from taking action on behalf of a national who is in prison, custody or detention if he expressly opposes such action.

2. The rights referred to in paragraph 1 of this Article shall be exercised in conformity with the laws and regulations of the receiving State, subject to the proviso, however, that the said laws and regulations must enable full effect to be given to the purposes for which the rights accorded under this Article are intended.

ARTICLE 37

Information in cases of deaths, guardianship or trusteeship, wrecks and air accidents

If the relevant information is available to the competent authorities of the receiving State, such authorities shall have the duty:

(a) in the case of the death of a national of the sending State, to inform without delay the consular post in whose district the death occurred;

(b) to inform the competent consular post without delay of any case where the appointment of a guardian or trustee appears to be in the interests of a minor or other person lacking full capacity who is a national of the sending State. The giving of this information shall, however, be without prejudice to the operation of the laws and regulations of the receiving State concerning such appointments;

(c) if a vessel, having the nationality of the sending State, is wrecked or runs aground in the territorial sea or internal waters of the receiving State, or if an aircraft registered in the sending State suffers an accident on the territory of the receiving State, to inform without delay the consular post nearest to the scene of the occurrence.

ARTICLE 38

Communication with the authorities of the receiving State

In the exercise of their functions, consular officers may address:

(a) the competent local authorities of their consular district;

(b) the competent central authorities of the receiving State if and to the extent that this is allowed by the laws, regulations and usages of the receiving State or by the relevant international agreements.

ARTICLE 39

Consular fees and charges

1. The consular post may levy in the territory of the receiving State the fees and charges provided by the laws and regulations of the sending State for consular acts.

2. The sums collected in the form of the fees and charges referred to in paragraph 1 of this Article, and the receipts for such fees and charges, shall be exempt from all dues and taxes in the receiving State.

SECTION II.—FACILITIES, PRIVILEGES AND IMMUNITIES RELATING TO CAREER CONSULAR OFFICERS AND OTHER MEMBERS OF A CONSULAR POST

ARTICLE 40

Protection of consular officers

The receiving State shall treat consular officers with due respect and shall take all appropriate steps to prevent any attack on their person, freedom or dignity.

ARTICLE 41

Personal inviolability of consular officers

1. Consular officers shall not be liable to arrest or detention pending trial, except in the case of a grave crime and pursuant to a decision by the competent judicial authority.

2. Except in the case specified in paragraph 1 of this Article, consular officers shall not be committed to prison or liable to any other form of restriction on their personal freedom save in execution of a judicial decision of final effect.

3. If criminal proceedings are instituted against a consular officer, he must appear before the competent authorities. Nevertheless, the proceedings shall be conducted with the respect due to him by reason of his official position and, except in the case specified in paragraph 1 of this Article, in a manner which will hamper the exercise of consular functions as little as possible. When, in the circumstances mentioned in paragraph 1 of this Article, it has become necessary to detain a consular officer, the proceedings against him shall be instituted with the minimum of delay.

ARTICLE 42

Notification of arrest, detention or prosecution

In the event of the arrest or detention, pending trial, of a member of the consular staff, or of criminal proceedings being instituted against him, the receiving State shall promptly notify the head of the consular post. Should the latter be himself the object of any such measure, the receiving State shall notify the sending State through the diplomatic channel.

94

ARTICLE 43

Immunity from jurisdiction

1. Consular officers and consular employees shall not be amenable to the jurisdiction of the judicial or administrative authorities of the receiving State in respect of acts performed in the exercise of consular functions.

2. The provisions of paragraph 1 of this Article shall not, however, apply in respect of a civil action either:

   (*a*) arising out of a contract concluded by a consular officer or a consular employee in which he did not contract expressly or impliedly as an agent of the sending State; or

   (*b*) by a third party for damage arising from an accident in the receiving State caused by a vehicle, vessel or aircraft.

ARTICLE 44

Liability to give evidence

1. Members of a consular post may be called upon to attend as witnesses in the course of judicial or administrative proceedings. A consular employee or a member of the service staff shall not, except in the cases mentioned in paragraph 3 of this Article, decline to give evidence. If a consular officer should decline to do so, no coercive measure or penalty may be applied to him.

2. The authority requiring the evidence of a consular officer shall avoid interference with the performance of his functions. It may, when possible, take such evidence at his residence or at the consular post or accept a statement from him in writing.

3. Members of a consular post are under no obligations to give evidence concerning matters connected with the exercise of their functions or to produce official correspondence and documents relating thereto. They are also entitled to decline to give evidence as expert witnesses with regard to the law of the sending State.

ARTICLE 45

Waiver of privileges and immunities

1. The sending State may waive, with regard to a member of the consular post, any of the privileges and immunities provided for in Articles 41, 43 and 44.

2. The waiver shall in all cases be express, except as provided in paragraph 3 of this Article, and shall be communicated to the receiving State in writing.

3. The initiation of proceedings by a consular officer or a consular employee in a matter where he might enjoy immunity from jurisdiction under Article 43 shall preclude him from invoking immunity from jurisdiction in respect of any counter-claim directly connected with the principal claim.

4. The waiver of immunity from jurisdiction for the purposes of civil

or administrative proceedings shall not be deemed to imply the waiver of immunity from the measures of execution resulting from the judicial decision; in respect of such measures, a separate waiver shall be necessary.

ARTICLE 46

Exemption from registration of aliens and residence permits

1. Consular officers and consular employees and members of their families forming part of their households shall be exempt from all obligations under the laws and regulations of the receiving State in regard to the registration of aliens and residence permits.

2. The provisions of paragraph 1 of this Article shall not, however, apply to any consular employee who is not a permanent employee of the sending State or who carries on any private gainful occupation in the receiving State or to any member of the family of any such employee.

ARTICLE 47

Exemption from work permits

1. Members of the consular post shall, with respect to services rendered for the sending State, be exempt from any obligations in regard to work permits imposed by the laws and regulations of the receiving State concerning the employment of foreign labour.

2. Members of the private staff of consular officers and of consular employees shall, if they do not carry on any other gainful occupation in the receiving State, be exempt from the obligations referred to in paragraph 1 of this Article.

ARTICLE 48

Social security exemption

1. Subject to the provisions of paragraph 3 of this Article, members of the consular post with respect to services rendered by them for the sending State, and members of their families forming part of their households, shall be exempt from social security provisions which may be in force in the receiving State.

2. The exemption provided for in paragraph 1 of this Article shall apply also to members of the private staff who are in the sole employ of members of the consular post, on condition:

(a) that they are not nationals of or permanently resident in the receiving State; and

(b) that they are covered by the social security provisions which are in force in the sending State or a third State.

3. Members of the consular post who employ persons to whom the exemption provided for in paragraph 2 of this Article does not apply shall observe the obligations which the social security provisions of the receiving State impose upon employers.

4. The exemption provided for in paragraphs 1 and 2 of this Article

shall not preclude voluntary participation in the social security system of the receiving State, provided that such participation is permitted by that State.

ARTICLE 49

Exemption from taxation

1. Consular officers and consular employees and members of their families forming part of their households shall be exempt from all dues and taxes, personal or real, national, regional or municipal, except:

(a) indirect taxes of a kind which are normally incorporated in the price of goods or services;
(b) dues or taxes on private immovable property situated in the territory of the receiving State, subject to the provisions of Article 32;
(c) estate, succession or inheritance duties, and duties on transfers, levied by the receiving State, subject to the provisions of paragraph (b) of Article 51;
(d) dues and taxes on private income, including capital gains, having its source in the receiving State and capital taxes relating to investments made in commercial or financial undertakings in the receiving State;
(e) charges levied for specific services rendered;
(f) registration, court or record fees, mortgage dues and stamp duties, subject to the provisions of Article 32.

2. Members of the service staff shall be exempt from dues and taxes on the wages which they receive for their services.

3. Members of the consular post who employ persons whose wages or salaries are not exempt from income tax in the receiving State shall observe the obligations which the laws and regulations of that State impose upon employers concerning the levying of income tax.

ARTICLE 50

Exemption from customs duties and inspection

1. The receiving State shall, in accordance with such laws and regulations as it may adopt, permit entry of and grant exemption from all customs duties, taxes, and related charges other than charges for storage, cartage and similar services, on:

(a) articles for the official use of the consular post;
(b) articles for the personal use of a consular officer or members of his family forming part of his household, including articles intended for his establishment. The articles intended for consumption shall not exceed the quantities necessary for direct utilization by the persons concerned.

2. Consular employees shall enjoy the privileges and exemptions specified in paragraph 1 of this Article in respect of articles imported at the time of first installation.

3. Personal baggage accompanying consular officers and members of their families forming part of their households shall be exempt from inspection. It may be inspected only if there is serious reason to believe that it contains articles other than those referred to in sub-paragraph (*b*) of paragraph 1 of this Article, or articles the import or export of which is prohibited by the laws and regulations of the receiving State or which are subject to its quarantine laws and regulations. Such inspection shall be carried out in the presence of the consular officer or member of his family concerned.

ARTICLE 51

Estate of a member of the consular post or of a member of his family

In the event of the death of a member of the consular post or of a member of his family forming part of his household, the receiving State:

(*a*) shall permit the export of the movable property of the deceased, with the exception of any such property acquired in the receiving State the export of which was prohibited at the time of his death;

(*b*) shall not levy national, regional or municipal estate, succession of inheritance duties, and duties on transfers, on movable property the presence of which in the receiving State was due solely to the presence in that State of the deceased as a member of the consular post or as a member of the family of a member of the consular post.

ARTICLE 52

Exemption from personal services and contributions

The receiving State shall exempt members of the consular post and members of their families forming part of their households from all personal services, from all public service of any kind whatsoever, and from military obligations such as those connected with requisitioning, military contributions and billeting.

ARTICLE 53

Beginning and end of consular privileges and immunities

1. Every member of the consular post shall enjoy the privileges and immunities provided in the present Convention from the moment he enters the territory of the receiving State on proceeding to take up his post or, if already in its territory, from the moment when he enters on his duties with the consular post.

2. Members of the family of a member of the consular post forming part of his household and members of his private staff shall receive the privileges and immunities provided in the present Convention from the date from which he enjoys privileges and immunities in accordance with paragraph 1 of this Article or from the date of their entry into the territory of the receiving State or from the date of their becoming a member of such family or private staff, whichever is the latest.

98

3. When the functions of a member of the consular post have come to an end, his privileges and immunities and those of a member of his family forming part of his household or a member of his private staff shall normally cease at the moment when the person concerned leaves the receiving State or on the expiry of a reasonable period in which to do so, whichever is the sooner, but shall subsist until that time, even in case of armed conflict. In the case of the persons referred to in paragraph 2 of this Article, their privileges and immunities shall come to an end when they cease to belong to the household or to be in the service of a member of the consular post provided, however, that if such persons intend leaving the receiving State within a reasonable period thereafter, their privileges and immunities shall subsist until the time of their departure.

4. However, with respect to acts performed by a consular officer or a consular employee in the exercise of his functions, immunity from jurisdiction shall continue to subsist without limitation of time.

5. In the event of the death of a member of the consular post, the members of his family forming part of his household shall continue to enjoy the privileges and immunities accorded to them until they leave the receiving State or until the expiry of a reasonable period enabling them to do so, whichever is the sooner.

ARTICLE 54

Obligations of third States

1. If a consular officer passes through or is in the territory of a third State, which has granted him a visa if a visa was necessary, while proceeding to take up or return to his post or when returning to the sending State, the third State shall accord to him all immunities provided for by the other Articles of the present Convention as may be required to ensure his transit or return. The same shall apply in the case of any member of his family forming part of his household enjoying such privileges and immunities who are accompanying the consular officer or travelling separately to join him or to return to the sending State.

2. In circumstances similar to those specified in paragraph 1 of this Article, third States shall not hinder the transit through their territory of other members of the consular post or of members of their families forming part of their households.

3. Third States shall accord to official correspondence and to other official communications in transit, including messages in code or cipher, the same freedom and protection as the receiving State is bound to accord under the present Convention. They shall accord to consular couriers who have been granted a visa, if a visa was necessary, and to consular bags in transit, the same inviolability and protection as the receiving State is bound to accord under the present Convention.

4. The obligations of third States under paragraphs 1, 2 and 3 of this Article shall also apply to the persons mentioned respectively in those paragraphs, and to official communications and to consular bags, whose presence in the territory of the third State is due to *force majeure*.

Respect for the laws and regulations of the receiving State

1. Without prejudice to their privileges and immunities, it is the duty of all persons enjoying such privileges and immunities to respect the laws and regulations of the receiving State. They also have a duty not to interfere in the internal affairs of that State.

2. The consular premises shall not be used in any manner incompatible with the exercise of consular functions.

3. The provisions of paragraph 2 of this Article shall not exclude the possibility of offices of other institutions or agencies being installed in part of the building in which the consular premises are situated, provided that the premises assigned to them are separate from those used by the consular post. In that event, the said offices shall not, for the purposes of the present Convention, be considered to form part of the consular premises.

Insurance against third party risks

Members of the consular post shall comply with any requirement imposed by the laws and regulations of the receiving State in respect of insurance against third party risks arising from the use of any vehicle, vessel or aircraft.

Special provisions concerning private gainful occupation

1. Career consular officers shall not carry on for personal profit any professional or commercial activity in the receiving State.

2. Privileges and immunities provided in this Chapter shall not be accorded:

(a) to consular employees or to members of the service staff who carry on any private gainful occupation in the receiving State;

(b) to members of the family of a person referred to in sub-paragraph (a) of this paragraph or to members of his private staff;

(c) to members of the family of a member of a consular post who themselves carry on any private gainful occupation in the receiving State.

CHAPTER III.—REGIME RELATING TO HONORARY CONSULAR OFFICERS AND CONSULAR POSTS HEADED BY SUCH OFFICERS

General provisions relating to facilities, privileges and immunities

1. Articles 28, 29, 30, 34, 35, 36, 37, 38 and 39, paragraph 3 of Article 54 and paragraphs 2 and 3 of Article 55 shall apply to consular posts headed

by an honorary consular officer. In addition, the facilities, privileges and immunities of such consular posts shall be governed by Articles 59, 60, 61 and 62.

2. Articles 42 and 43, paragraph 3 of Article 44, Articles 45 and 53 and paragraph 1 of Article 55 shall apply to honorary consular officers. In addition, the facilities, privileges and immunities of such consular officers shall be governed by Articles 63, 64, 65, 66 and 67.

3. Privileges and immunities provided in the present Convention shall not be accorded to members of the family of an honorary consular officer or of a consular employee employed at a consular post headed by an honorary consular officer.

4. The exchange of consular bags between two consular posts headed by honorary consular officers in different States shall not be allowed without the consent of the two receiving States concerned.

ARTICLE 59

Protection of the consular premises

The receiving State shall take such steps as may be necessary to protect the consular premises of a consular post headed by an honorary consular officer against any intrusion or damage and to prevent any disturbance of the peace of the consular post or impairment of its dignity.

ARTICLE 60

Exemption from taxation of consular premises

1. Consular premises of a consular post headed by an honorary consular officer of which the sending State is the owner or lessee shall be exempt from all national, regional or municipal dues and taxes whatsoever, other than such as represent payment for specific services rendered.

2. The exemption from taxation referred to in paragraph 1 of this Article shall not apply to such dues and taxes if, under the laws and regulations of the receiving State, they are payable by the person who contracted with the sending State.

ARTICLE 61

Inviolability of consular archives and documents

The consular archives and documents of a consular post headed by an honorary consular officer shall be inviolable at all times and wherever they may be, provided that they are kept separate from other papers and documents and, in particular, from the private correspondence of the head of a consular post and of any person working with him, and from the materials, books or documents relating to their profession or trade.

ARTICLE 62

Exemption from customs duties

The receiving State shall, in accordance with such laws and regulations as it may adopt, permit entry of, and grant exemption from all customs

H

duties, taxes, and related charges other than charges for storage, cartage and similar services on the following articles, provided that they are for the official use of a consular post headed by an honorary consular officer: coats-of-arms, flags, signboards, seals and stamps, books, official printed matter, office furniture, office equipment and similar articles supplied by or at the instance of the sending State to the consular post.

ARTICLE 63

Criminal proceedings

If criminal proceedings are instituted against an honorary consular officer, he must appear before the competent authorities. Nevertheless, the proceedings shall be conducted with the respect due to him by reason of his official position and, except when he is under arrest or detention, in a manner which will hamper the exercise of consular functions as little as possible. When it has become necessary to detain an honorary consular officer, the proceedings against him shall be instituted with the minimum of delay.

ARTICLE 64

Protection of honorary consular officers

The receiving State is under a duty to accord to an honorary consular officer such protection as may be required by reason of his official position.

ARTICLE 65

Exemption from registration of aliens and residence permits

Honorary consular officers, with the exception of those who carry on for personal profit any professional or commercial activity in the receiving State, shall be exempt from all obligations under the laws and regulations of the receiving State in regard to the registration of aliens and residence permits.

ARTICLE 66

Exemption from taxation

An honorary consular officer shall be exempt from all dues and taxes on the remuneration and emoluments which he receives from the sending State in respect of the exercise of consular functions.

ARTICLE 67

Exemption from personal services and contributions

The receiving State shall exempt honorary consular officers from all personal services and from all public services of any kind whatsoever and from military obligations such as those connected with requisitioning, military contributions and billeting.

ARTICLE 68

Optional character of the institution of honorary consular officers

Each State is free to decide whether it will appoint or receive honorary consular officers.

CHAPTER IV.—GENERAL PROVISIONS

ARTICLE 69

Consular agents who are not heads of consular posts

1. Each State is free to decide whether it will establish or admit consular agencies conducted by consular agents not designated as heads of consular post by the sending State.

2. The conditions under which the consular agencies referred to in paragraph 1 of this Article may carry on their activities and the privileges and immunities which may be enjoyed by the consular agents in charge of them shall be determined by agreement between the sending State and the receiving State.

ARTICLE 70

Exercise of consular functions by diplomatic missions

1. The provisions of the present Convention apply also, so far as the context permits, to the exercise of consular functions by a diplomatic mission.

2. The names of members of a diplomatic mission assigned to the consular section or otherwise charged with the exercise of the consular functions of the mission shall be notified to the Ministry for Foreign Affairs of the receiving State or to the authority designated by that Ministry.

3. In the exercise of consular functions a diplomatic mission may address:

(*a*) the local authorities of the consular district;
(*b*) the central authorities of the receiving State if this is allowed by the laws, regulations and usages of the receiving State or by relevant international agreements.

4. The privileges and immunities of the members of a diplomatic mission referred to in paragraph 2 of this Article shall continue to be governed by the rules of international law concerning diplomatic relations.

ARTICLE 71

Nationals or permanent residents of the receiving State

1. Except in so far as additional facilities, privileges and immunities may be granted by the receiving State, consular officers who are nationals of or permanently resident in the receiving State shall enjoy only immunity from jurisdiction and personal inviolability in respect of official acts performed in the exercise of their functions, and the privilege provided

in paragraph 3 of Article 44. So far as these consular officers are concerned, the receiving State shall likewise be bound by the obligation laid down in Article 42. If criminal proceedings are instituted against such a consular officer, the proceedings shall, except when he is under arrest or detention, be conducted in a manner which will hamper the exercise of consular functions as little as possible.

2. Other members of the consular post who are nationals of or permanently resident in the receiving State and members of their families, as well as members of the families of consular officers referred to in paragraph 1 of this Article, shall enjoy facilities, privileges and immunities only in so far as these are granted to them by the receiving State. Those members of the families of members of the consular post and those members of the private staff who are themselves nationals of or permanently resident in the receiving State shall likewise enjoy facilities, privileges and immunities only in so far as these are granted to them by the receiving State. The receiving State shall, however, exercise its jurisdiction over those persons in such a way as not to hinder unduly the performance of the functions of the consular post.

ARTICLE 72

Non-discrimination

1. In the application of the provisions of the present Convention the receiving State shall not discriminate as between States.

2. However, discrimination shall not be regarded as taking place:

(a) where the receiving State applies any of the provisions of the present Convention restrictively because of a restrictive application of that provision to its consular posts in the sending State;

(b) where by custom or agreement States extend to each other more favourable treatment than is required by the provisions of the present Convention.

ARTICLE 73

Relationship between the present Convention and other international agreements

1. The provisions of the present Convention shall not affect other international agreements in force as between States parties to them.

2. Nothing in the present Convention shall preclude States from concluding international agreements confirming or supplementing or extending or amplifying the provisions thereof.

CHAPTER V.—FINAL PROVISIONS

ARTICLE 74

Signature

The present Convention shall be open for signature by all States Members of the United Nations or of any of the specialised agencies or Parties

104

to the Statute of the International Court of Justice, and by any other State invited by the General Assembly of the United Nations to become a Party to the Convention, as follows: until 31 October 1963 at the Federal Ministry for Foreign Affairs of the Republic of Austria and subsequently, until 31 March 1964, at the United Nations Headquarters in New York.

ARTICLE 75

Ratification

The present Convention is subject to ratification. The instruments of ratification shall be deposited with the Secretary-General of the United Nations.

ARTICLE 76

Accession

The present Convention shall remain open for accession by any State belonging to any of the four categories mentioned in Article 74. The instruments of accession shall be deposited with the Secretary-General of the United Nations.

ARTICLE 77

Entry into force

1. The present Convention shall enter into force on the thirtieth day following the date of deposit of the twenty-second instrument of ratification or accession with the Secretary-General of the United Nations.

2. For each State ratifying or acceding to the Convention after the deposit of the twenty-second instrument of ratification or accession, the Convention shall enter into force on the thirtieth day after deposit by such State of its instrument of ratification or accession.

ARTICLE 78

Notifications by the Secretary-General

The Secretary-General of the United Nations shall inform all States belonging to any of the four categories mentioned in Article 74:

(a) of signatures to the present Convention and of the deposit of instruments of ratification or accession, in accordance with Articles 74, 75 and 76;

(b) of the date on which the present Convention will enter into force in accordance with Article 77.

ARTICLE 79

Authentic texts

The original of the present Convention, of which the Chinese, English, French, Russian and Spanish texts are equally authentic, shall be deposited with the Secretary-General of the United Nations, who shall send certified copies thereof to all States belonging to any of the four categories mentioned in Article 74.

IN WITNESS WHEREOF the undersigned Plenipotentiaries, being duly authorized thereto by their respective Governments, have signed the present Convention.

DONE AT VIENNA, this twenty-fourth day of April, one thousand nine hundred and sixty-three.

Appendix 4

CONVENTION ON TRANSIT TRADE OF LAND-LOCKED STATES

8 July 1965

PREAMBLE

The States Parties to the present Convention,

Recalling that article 55 of its Charter requires the United Nations to promote conditions of economic progress and solutions of international economic problems,

Noting General Assembly resolution 1028 (XI) on the land-locked countries and the expansion of international trade which, 'recognising the need of land-locked countries for adequate transit facilities in promoting international trade', invited 'the Governments of Member States to give full recognition to the needs of land-locked Member States in the matter of transit trade and, therefore, to accord them adequate facilities in terms of international law and practice in this regard, bearing in mind the future requirements resulting from the economic development of the land-locked countries',

Recalling article 2 of the Convention on the High Seas which states that the high seas being open to all nations, no State may validly purport to subject any part of them to its sovereignty and article 3 of the said Convention which states:

'1. In order to enjoy the freedom of the seas on equal terms with coastal States, States having no sea-coast should have free access to the sea. To this end States situated between the sea and a State having no sea-coast shall by common agreement with the latter and in conformity with existing international conventions accord:

(a) To the State having no sea-coast, on a basis of reciprocity, free transit through their territory; and

(b) To ships flying the flag of that State treatment equal to that accorded to their own ships, or to the ships of any other States, as regards access to seaports and the use of such ports.'

'2. States situated between the sea and a State having no sea-coast shall settle, by mutual agreement with the latter, and taking into account the rights of the coastal State or State of transit and the special conditions of the State having no sea-coast, all matters relating to freedom of transit and equal treatment in ports, in case such States are not already parties to existing international conventions.'

107

Reaffirming the following principles adopted by the United Nations Conference on Trade and Development with the understanding that these principles are inter-related and each principle should be construed in the context of the other principles:

Principle I

The recognition of the right of each land-locked State of free access to the sea is an essential principle for the expansion of international trade and economic development.

Principle II

In territorial and on internal waters, vessels flying the flag of land-locked countries should have identical rights and enjoy treatment identical to that enjoyed by vessels flying the flag of coastal States other than the territorial State.

Principle III

In order to enjoy the freedom of the seas on equal terms with coastal States, States having no sea-coast should have free access to the sea. To this end States situated between the sea and a State having no sea-coast shall by common agreement with the latter and in conformity with existing international conventions accord to ships flying the flag of that State treatment equal to that accorded to their own ships or to the ships of any other State as regards access to seaports and the use of such ports.

Principle IV

In order to promote fully the economic development of the land-locked countries, the said countries should be afforded by all States, on the basis of reciprocity, free and unrestricted transit, in such a manner that they have free access to regional and international trade in all circumstances and for every type of goods.

Goods in transit should not be subject to any customs duty.

Means of transport in transit should not be subject to special taxes or charges higher than those levied for the use of means of transport of the transit country.

Principle V

The State of transit, while maintaining full sovereignty over its territory, shall have the right to take all indispensable measures to ensure that the exercise of the right of free and unrestricted transit shall in no way infringe its legitimate interests of any kind.

Principle VI

In order to accelerate the evolution of a universal approach to the solution of the special and particular problems of trade and development of land-locked countries in the different geographical areas, the conclusion of regional and other international agreements in this regard should be encouraged by all States.

Principle VII

The facilities and special rights accorded to land-locked countries in view of their special geographical position are excluded from the operation of the most-favoured-nation clause.

Principle VIII

The principles which govern the right of free access to the sea of the land-locked State shall in no way abrogate existing agreements between two or more contracting parties concerning the problems, nor shall they raise an obstacle as regards the conclusions of such agreements in the future, provided that the latter do not establish a regime which is less favourable than or opposed to the above-mentioned provisions.

Have agreed as follows:

ARTICLE 1

Definitions

For the purpose of this Convention,

(*a*) the term 'land-locked State' means any Contracting State which has no sea-coast;

(*b*) the term 'traffic in transit' means the passage of goods including unaccompanied baggage across the territory of a Contracting State between a land-locked State and the sea when the passage is a portion of a complete journey which begins or terminates within the territory of that land-locked State and which includes sea transport directly preceding or following such passage. The trans-shipment, warehousing, breaking bulk, and change in the mode of transport of such goods as well as the assembly, disassembly or reassembly of machinery and bulky goods shall not render the passage of goods outside the definition of 'traffic in transit' provided that any such operation is undertaken solely for the convenience of transportation. Nothing in this paragraph shall be construed as imposing an obligation on any Contracting State to establish or permit the establishment of permanent facilities on its territory for such assembly, disassembly or reassembly;

(*c*) the term 'transit State' means any Contracting State with or without a sea-coast, situated between a land-locked State and the sea, through whose territory 'traffic in transit' passes;

(*d*) the term 'means of transport' includes:

(i) any railway stock, seagoing and river vessels and road vehicles;

(ii) where the local situation so requires porters and pack animals;

(iii) if agreed upon by the Contracting States concerned, other means of transport and pipelines and gas lines

when they are used for traffic in transit within the meaning of this article.

ARTICLE 2

Freedom of transit

1. Freedom of transit shall be granted under the terms of this Convention for traffic in transit and means of transport. Subject to the other provisions of this Convention, the measures taken by Contracting States for regulating and forwarding traffic across their territory shall facilitate traffic in transit on routes in use mutually acceptable for transit to the Contracting States concerned. Consistent with the terms of this Convention, no discrimination shall be exercised which is based on the place of origin, departure, entry, exit or destination or on any circumstances relating to the ownership of the goods or the ownership, place of registration or flag of vessels, land vehicles or other means of transport used.

2. The rules governing the use of means of transport, when they pass across part or the whole of the territory of another Contracting State, shall be established by common agreement among the Contracting States concerned, with due regard to the multilateral international conventions to which these States are parties.

3. Each Contracting State shall authorise, in accordance with its laws, rules and regulations, the passage across or access to its territory of persons whose movement is necessary for traffic in transit.

4. The Contracting States shall permit the passage of traffic in transit across their territorial waters in accordance with the principles of customary international law or applicable international conventions and with their internal regulations.

ARTICLE 3

Customs duties and special transit dues

Traffic in transit shall not be subjected by any authority within the transit State to customs duties or taxes chargeable by reason of importation or exportation nor to any special dues in respect of transit. Nevertheless on such traffic in transit there may be levied charges intended solely to defray expenses of supervision and administration entailed by such transit. The rate of any such charges must correspond as nearly as possible with the expenses they are intended to cover and, subject to that condition, the charges must be imposed in conformity with the requirement of non-discrimination laid down in article 2, paragraph 1.

ARTICLE 4

Means of transport and tariffs

1. The Contracting States undertake to provide, subject to availability, at the points of entry and exit, and as required at points of trans-shipment, adequate means of transport and handling equipment for the movement of traffic in transit without unnecessary delay.

2. The Contracting States undertake to apply to traffic in transit, using facilities operated or administered by the State, tariffs or charges which, having regard to the conditions of the traffic and to considerations of

commercial competition, are reasonable as regards both their rates and the method of their application. These tariffs or charges shall be so fixed as to facilitate traffic in transit as much as possible, and shall not be higher than the tariffs or charges applied by Contracting States for the transport through their territory of goods of countries with access to the sea. The provisions of this paragraph shall also extend to the tariffs and charges applicable to traffic in transit using facilities operated or administered by firms or individuals, in cases in which the tariffs or charges are fixed or subject to control by the Contracting State. The term 'facilities' used in this paragraph shall comprise means of transport, port installations and routes for the use of which tariffs or charges are levied.

3. Any haulage service etablished as a monopoly on waterways used for transit must be so organized as not to hinder the transit of vessels.

4. The provisions of this article must be applied under the conditions of non-discrimination laid down in article 2, paragraph 1.

ARTICLE 5

Methods and documentation in regard to customs, transport, etc.

1. The Contracting States shall apply administrative and customs measures permitting the carrying out of free, uninterrupted and continuous traffic in transit. When necessary, they should undertake negotiations to agree on measures that ensure and facilitate the said transit.

2. The Contracting States undertake to use simplified documentation and expeditious methods in regard to customs, transport and other administrative procedures relating to traffic in transit for the whole transit journey on their territory, including any trans-shipment, warehousing, breaking bulk, and changes in the mode of transport as may take place in the course of such journey.

ARTICLE 6

Storage of goods in transit

1. The conditions of storage of goods in transit at the points of entry and exit, and at intermediate stages in the transit State may be established by agreement between the States concerned. The transit States shall grant conditions of storage at least as favourable as those granted to goods coming from or going to their own countries.

2. The tariffs and charges shall be established in accordance with article 4.

ARTICLE 7

Delays or difficulties in traffic in transit

1. Except in cases of *force majeure* all measures shall be taken by Contracting States to avoid delays in or restrictions on traffic in transit.

2. Should delays or other difficulties occur in traffic in transit, the competent authorities of the transit State or States and of the land-locked State shall co-operate towards their expeditious elimination.

ARTICLE 8

Free zones or other customs facilities

1. For convenience of traffic in transit, free zones or other customs facilities may be provided at the ports of entry and exit in the transit States, by agreement between those States and the land-locked States.

2. Facilities of this nature may also be provided for the benefit of land-locked States in other transit States which have no sea-coast or seaports.

ARTICLE 9

Provision of greater facilities

This Convention does not entail in any way the withdrawal of transit facilities which are greater than those provided for in the Convention and which under conditions consistent with its principles, are agreed between Contracting States or granted by a Contracting State. The Convention also does not preclude such grant of greater facilities in the future.

ARTICLE 10

Relation to most-favoured-nation clause

1. The Contracting States agree that the facilities and special rights accorded by this Convention to land-locked States in view of their special geographical position are excluded from the operation of the most-favoured-nation clause. A land-locked State which is not a Party to this Convention may claim the facilities and special rights accorded to land-locked States under this Convention only on the basis of the most-favoured-nation clause of a treaty between that land-locked State and the Contracting State granting such facilities and special rights.

2. If a Contracting State grants to a land-locked State facilities or special rights greater than those provided for in this Convention, such facilities or special rights may be limited to that land-locked State, except in so far as the withholding of such greater facilities or special rights from any other land-locked State contravenes the most-favoured-nation provision of a treaty between such other land-locked State and the Contracting State granting such facilities or special rights.

ARTICLE 11

Exceptions to Convention on grounds of public health, security, and protection of intellectual property

1. No Contracting State shall be bound by this Convention to afford transit to persons whose admission into its territory is forbidden, or for goods of a kind of which the importation is prohibited, either on grounds of public morals, public health or security, or as a precaution against diseases of animals or plants or against pests.

2. Each Contracting State shall be entitled to take reasonable precautions and measures to ensure that persons and goods, particularly goods which are the subject of a monopoly, are really in transit, and that

the means of transport are really used for the passage of such goods, as well as to protect the safety of the routes and means of communication.

3. Nothing in this Convention shall affect the measures which a Contracting State may be called upon to take in pursuance of provisions in a general international convention, whether of a world-wide or regional character, to which it is a party, whether such convention was already concluded on the date of this Convention or is concluded later, when such provisions relate:

(a) to export or import or transit of particular kinds of articles such as narcotics, or other dangerous drugs, or arms; or

(b) to protection of industrial, literary or artistic property, or protection of trade names, and indications of source or appellations of origin, and the suppression of unfair competition.

4. Nothing in this Convention shall prevent any Contracting State from taking any action necessary for the protection of its essential security interests.

ARTICLE 12

Exceptions in case of emergency

The measures of a general or particular character which a Contracting State is obliged to take in case of an emergency endangering its political existence or its safety may, in exceptional cases and for as short a period as possible, involve a deviation from the provisions of this Convention on the understanding that the principle of freedom of transit shall be observed to the utmost possible extent during such a period.

ARTICLE 13

Application of the Convention in time of war

This Convention does not prescribe the rights and duties of belligerents and neutrals in time of war. The Convention shall, however, continue in force in time of war so far as such rights and duties permit.

ARTICLE 14

Obligations under the Convention and rights and duties of United Nations Members

This Convention does not impose upon a Contracting State any obligation conflicting with its rights and duties as a Member of the United Nations.

ARTICLE 15

Reciprocity

The provisions of this Convention shall be applied on a basis of reciprocity.

ARTICLE 16

Settlement of disputes

1. Any dispute which may arise with respect to the interpretation or application of the provisions of this Convention which is not settled by negotiation or by other peaceful means of settlement within a period of nine months shall, at the request of either party, be settled by arbitration. The arbitration commission shall be composed of three members. Each party to the dispute shall appoint one member to the commission, while the third member, who shall be the Chairman, shall be chosen in common agreement between the parties. If the parties fail to agree on the designation of the third member within a period of three months, the third member shall be appointed by the President of the International Court of Justice. In case any of the parties fail to make an appointment within a period of three months the President of the International Court of Justice shall fill the remaining vacancy or vacancies.

2. The arbitration commission shall decide on the matters placed before it by simple majority and its decisions shall be binding on the parties.

3. Arbitration commissions or other international bodies charged with settlement of disputes under this Convention shall inform, through the Secretary-General of the United Nations, the other Contracting States of the existence and nature of disputes and of the terms of their settlement.

ARTICLE 17

Signature

The present Convention shall be open until 31 December 1965 for signature by all States Members of the United Nations or of any of the specialised agencies or Parties to the Statute of the International Court of Justice, and by any other State invited by the General Assembly of the United Nations to become a Party to the Convention.

ARTICLE 18

Ratification

The present Convention is subject to ratification. The instruments of ratification shall be deposited with the Secretary-General of the United Nations.

ARTICLE 19

Accession

The present Convention shall remain open for accession by any State belonging to any of the four categories mentioned in article 17. The instruments of accession shall be deposited with the Secretary-General of the United Nations.

APPENDIX 4

ARTICLE 20

Entry into force

1. The present Convention shall enter into force on the thirtieth day following the date of deposit of the instruments of ratification or accession of at least two land-locked States and two transit States having a sea coast.

2. For each State ratifying or acceding to the Convention after the deposit of the instruments of ratification or accession necessary for the entry into force of this Convention in accordance with paragraph 1 of this article, the Convention shall enter into force on the thirtieth day after the deposit by such State of its instrument of ratification or accession.

ARTICLE 21

Revision

At the request of one-third of the Contracting States, and with the concurrence of the majority of the Contracting States, the Secretary-General of the United Nations shall convene a Conference with a view to the revision of this Convention.

ARTICLE 22

Notifications by the Secretary-General

The Secretary-General of the United Nations shall inform all States belonging to any of the four categories mentioned in article 17;

(a) of signatures to the present Convention and of the deposit of instruments of ratification or accession, in accordance with articles 17, 18 and 19;

(b) of the date on which the present Convention will enter into force, in accordance with article 20;

(c) of requests for revision, in accordance with article 21.

ARTICLE 23

Authentic texts

The original of the present Convention, of which the Chinese, English, French, Russian and Spanish texts are equally authentic, shall be deposited with the Secretary-General of the United Nations, who shall send certified copies thereof to all States belonging to any of the four categories mentioned in article 17.

115

Appendix 5

INTERNATIONAL COVENANT ON ECONOMIC, SOCIAL AND CULTURAL RIGHTS

16 December 1966

PREAMBLE

The States Parties to the present Covenant,

Considering that, in accordance with the principles proclaimed in the Charter of the United Nations, recognition of the inherent dignity and of the equal and inalienable rights of all members of the human family is the foundation of freedom, justice and peace in the world,

Recognising that these rights derive from the inherent dignity of the human person,

Recognising that, in accordance with the Universal Declaration of Human Rights, the ideal of free human beings enjoying freedom from fear and want can only be achieved if conditions are created whereby everyone may enjoy his economic, social and cultural rights, as well as his civil and political rights,

Considering the obligation of States under the Charter of the United Nations to promote universal respect for, and observance of, human rights and freedoms,

Realising that the individual, having duties to other individuals and to the community to which he belongs, is under a responsibility to strive for the promotion and observance of the rights recognised in the present Covenant,

Agree upon the following articles:

PART I

ARTICLE 1

1. All peoples have the right of self-determination. By virtue of that right they freely determine their political status and freely pursue their economic, social and cultural development.

2. All peoples may, for their own ends, freely dispose of their natural wealth and resources without prejudice to any obligations arising out of international economic co-operation, based upon the principle of mutual benefit, and international law. In no case may a people be deprived of its own means of subsistence.

3. The States Parties to the present Covenant, including those having

responsibility for the administration of Non-Self-Governing and Trust Territories shall promote the realisation of the right of self-determination, and shall respect that right, in conformity with the provisions of the Charter of the United Nations.

PART II

ARTICLE 2

1. Each State Party to the present Covenant undertakes to take steps, individually and through international assistance and co-operation, especially economic and technical, to the maximum of its available resources, with a view to achieving progressively the full realisation of the rights recognised in the present Covenant by all appropriate means, including particularly the adoption of legislative measures.

2. The States Parties to the present Covenant undertake to guarantee that the rights enunciated in the present Covenant will be exercised without discrimination of any kind as to race, colour, sex, language, religion, political or other opinion, national or social origin, property, birth or other status.

3. Developing countries, with due regard to human rights and their national economy, may determine to what extent they would guarantee the economic rights recognised in the present Covenant to non-nationals.

ARTICLE 3

The States Parties to the present Covenant undertake to ensure the equal right of men and women to the enjoyment of all economic, social and cultural rights set forth in the present Covenant.

ARTICLE 4

The States Parties to the present Covenant recognise that, in the enjoyment of those rights provided by the State in conformity with the present Covenant, the State may subject such rights only to such limitations as are determined by law only in so far as this may be compatible with the nature of these rights and solely for the purpose of promoting the general welfare in a democratic society.

ARTICLE 5

1. Nothing in the present Covenant may be interpreted as implying for any State, group or person any right to engage in any activity or to perform any act aimed at the destruction of any of the rights or freedoms recognised herein, or at their limitation to a greater extent than is provided for in the present Covenant.

2. No restriction upon or derogation from any of the fundamental human rights recognised or existing in any country in virtue of law, conventions, regulations or custom shall be admitted on the pretext that the present Covenant does not recognise such rights or that it recognises them to a lesser extent.

PART III

ARTICLE 6

1. The States Parties to the present Covenant recognise the right to work, which includes the right of everyone to the opportunity to gain his living by work which he freely chooses or accepts, and will take appropriate steps to safeguard this right.

2. The steps to be taken by a State Party to the present Covenant to achieve the full realisation of this right shall include technical and vocational guidance and training programmes, policies and techniques to achieve steady economic, social and cultural development and full and productive employment under conditions safeguarding fundamental political and economic freedoms to the individual.

ARTICLE 7

The States Parties to the present Covenant recognise the right of everyone to the enjoyment of just and favourable conditions of work, which ensure, in particular:

(a) Remuneration which provides all workers, as a minimum, with:
    (i) Fair wages and equal remuneration for work of equal value without distinction of any kind, in particular women being guaranteed conditions of work not inferior to those enjoyed by men, with equal pay for equal work;
    (ii) A decent living for themselves and their families in accordance with the provisions of the present Covenant;

(b) Safe and healthy working conditions;

(c) Equal opportunity for everyone to be promoted in his employment to an appropriate higher level, subject to no considerations other than those of seniority and competence;

(d) Rest, leisure and reasonable limitation of working hours and periodic holidays with pay, as well as remuneration for public holidays.

ARTICLE 8

1. The States Parties to the present Covenant undertake to ensure:

(a) The right of everyone to form trade unions and join the trade union of his choice, subject only to the rules of the organisation concerned, for the promotion and protection of his economic and social interests. No restrictions may be placed on the exercise of this right other than those prescribed by law and which are necessary in a democratic society in the interests of national security or public order or for the protection of the rights and freedoms of others;

(b) The right of trade unions to establish national federations or confederations and the right of the latter to form or join international trade union organizations;

(c) The right of trade unions to function freely subject to no limitations other than those prescribed by law and which are necessary in a democratic society in the interests of national security or public order or for the protection of the rights and freedoms of others;

(*d*) The right to strike, provided that it is exercised in conformity with the laws of the particular country.

2. This article shall not prevent the imposition of lawful restrictions on the exercise of these rights by members of the armed forces or of the police or of the administration of the State.

3. Nothing in this article shall authorise States Parties to the International Labour Organisation Convention of 1948 concerning Freedom of Association and Protection of the Right to Organise to take legislative measures which would prejudice, or apply the law in such a manner as would prejudice, the guarantees provided for in that Convention.

ARTICLE 9

The States Parties to the present Covenant recognise the right of everyone to social security, including social insurance.

ARTICLE 10

The States Parties to the present Covenant recognise that:

1. The widest possible protection and assistance should be accorded to the family, which is the natural and fundamental group unit of society, particularly for its establishment and while it is responsible for the care and education of dependent children. Marriage must be entered into with the free consent of the intending spouses.
2. Special protection should be accorded to mothers during a reasonable period before and after childbirth. During such period working mothers should be accorded paid leave or leave with adequate social security benefits.
3. Special measures of protection and assistance should be taken on behalf of all children and young persons without any discrimination for reasons of parentage or other conditions. Children and young persons should be protected from economic and social exploitation. Their employment in work harmful to their morals or health or dangerous to life or likely to hamper their normal development should be punishable by law. States should also set age limits below which the paid employment of child labour should be prohibited and punishable by law.

ARTICLE 11

1. The States Parties to the present Covenant recognise the right of everyone to an adequate standard of living for himself and his family, including adequate food, clothing and housing, and to the continuous improvement of living conditions. The States Parties will take appropriate steps to ensure the realisation of this right, recognising to this effect the essential importance of international co-operation based on free consent.

2. The States Parties to the present Covenant, recognising the fundamental right of everyone to be free from hunger, shall take, individually and through international co-operation, the measures, including specific programmes, which are needed:

(*a*) To improve methods of production, conservation and distribution of food by making full use of technical and scientific knowledge, by disseminating knowledge of the principles of nutrition and by developing or reforming agrarian systems in such a way as to achieve the most efficient development and utilisation of natural resources;

(b) Taking into account the problems of both food-importing and food-exporting countries, to ensure an equitable distribution of world food supplies in relation to need.

ARTICLE 12

1. The States Parties to the present Covenant recognise the right of everyone to the enjoyment of the highest attainable standard of physical and mental health.

2. The steps to be taken by the States Parties to the present Covenant to achieve the full realisation of this right shall include those necessary for:

(a) The provision for the reduction of the stillbirth-rate and of infant mortality and for the healthy development of the child;

(b) The improvement of all aspects of environmental and industrial hygiene;

(c) The prevention, treatment and control of epidemic, endemic, occupational and other diseases;

(d) The creation of conditions which would assure to all medical service and medical attention in the event of sickness.

ARTICLE 13

1. The States Parties to the present Covenant recognise the right of everyone to education. They agree that education shall be directed to the full development of the human personality and the sense of its dignity, and shall strengthen the respect for human rights and fundamental freedoms. They further agree that education shall enable all persons to participate effectively in a free society, promote understanding, tolerance and friendship among all nations and all racial, ethnic or religious groups, and further the activities of the United Nations for the maintenance of peace.

2. The States Parties to the present Covenant recognise that, with a view to achieving the full realisation of this right:

(a) Primary education shall be compulsory and available free to all;

(b) Secondary education in its different forms, including technical and vocational secondary education, shall be made generally available and accessible to all by every appropriate means, and in particular by the progressive introduction of free education;

(c) Higher education shall be made equally accessible to all, on the basis of capacity, by every appropriate means, and in particular by the progressive introduction of free education;

(d) Fundamental education shall be encouraged or intensified as far as possible for those persons who have not received or completed the whole period of their primary education;

(e) The development of a system of schools at all levels shall be actively pursued, an adequate fellowship system shall be established, and the material conditions of teaching staff shall be continuously improved.

120

3. The States Parties to the present Covenant undertake to have respect for the liberty of parents and, when applicable, legal guardians, to choose for their children schools, other than those established by the public authorities, which conform to such minimum educational standards as may be laid down or approved by the State and to ensure the religious and moral education of their children in conformity with their own convictions.

4. No part of this article shall be construed so as to interfere with the liberty of individuals and bodies to establish and direct educational institutions, subject always to the observance of the principles set forth in paragraph 1 of this article and to the requirement that the education given in such institutions shall conform to such minimum standards as may be laid down by the State.

ARTICLE 14

Each State Party to the present Covenant which, at the time of becoming a Party, has not been able to secure in its metropolitan territory or other territories under its jurisdiction compulsory primary education, free of charge, undertakes, within two years, to work out and adopt a detailed plan of action for the progressive implementation, within a reasonable number of years, to be fixed in the plan, of the principle of compulsory education free of charge for all.

ARTICLE 15

1. The States Parties to the present Covenant recognise the right of everyone:

(a) To take part in cultural life;
(b) To enjoy the benefits of scientific progress and its applications;
(c) To benefit from the protection of the moral and material interests resulting from any scientific, literary or artistic production of which he is the author.

2. The steps to be taken by the States Parties to the present Covenant to achieve the full realisation of this right shall include those necessary for the conservation, the development and the diffusion of science and culture.

3. The States Parties to the present Covenant undertake to respect the freedom indispensable for scientific research and creative activity.

4. The States Parties to the present Covenant recognise the benefits to be derived from the encouragement and development of international contacts and co-operation in the scientific and cultural fields.

PART IV

ARTICLE 16

1. The States Parties to the present Covenant undertake to submit in conformity with this part of the Covenant reports on the measures which they have adopted and the progress made in achieving the observance of the rights recognised herein.

2. (a) All reports shall be submitted to the Secretary-General of the United Nations, who shall transmit copies to the Economic and Social

Council for consideration in accordance with the provisions of the present Covenant.

(*b*) The Secretary-General of the United Nations shall also transmit to the specialised agencies copies of the reports, or any relevant parts therefrom, from States Parties to the present Covenant which are also members of these specialised agencies in so far as these reports, or parts therefrom, relate to any matters which fall within the responsibilities of the said agencies in accordance with their constitutional instruments.

ARTICLE 17

1. The States Parties to the present Covenant shall furnish their reports in stages, in accordance with a programme to be established by the Economic and Social Council within one year of the entry into force of the present Covenant after consultation with the States Parties and the specialised agencies concerned.

2. Reports may indicate factors and difficulties affecting the degree of fulfilment of obligations under the present Covenant.

3. Where relevant information has previously been furnished to the United Nations or to any specialised agency by any State Party to the present Covenant, it will not be necessary to reproduce that information, but a precise reference to the information so furnished will suffice.

ARTICLE 18

Pursuant to its responsibilities under the Charter of the United Nations in the field of human rights and fundamental freedoms, the Economic and Social Council may make arrangements with the specialised agencies in respect of their reporting to it on the progress made in achieving the observance of the provisions of the present Covenant falling within the scope of their activities. These reports may include particulars of decisions and recommendations on such implementation adopted by their competent organs.

ARTICLE 19

The Economic and Social Council may transmit to the Commission on Human Rights for study and general recommendation or as appropriate for information the reports concerning human rights submitted by States in accordance with articles 16 and 17, and those concerning human rights submitted by the specialised agencies in accordance with article 18.

ARTICLE 20

The States Parties to the present Covenant and the specialised agencies concerned may submit comments to the Economic and Social Council on any general recommendation under article 19 or reference to such general recommendation in any report of the Commission on Human Rights or any documentation referred to therein.

ARTICLE 21

The Economic and Social Council may submit from time to time to the General Assembly reports with recommendations of a general nature and a

APPENDIX 5

summary of the information received from the States Parties to the present Covenant and the specialised agencies on the measures taken and the progress made in achieving general observance of the rights recognised in the present Covenant.

ARTICLE 22

The Economic and Social Council may bring to the attention of other organs of the United Nations, their subsidiary organs and specialised agencies concerned with furnishing technical assistance any matters arising out of the reports referred to in this part of the present Covenant which may assist such bodies in deciding, each within its field of competence, on the advisability of international measures likely to contribute to the effective progressive implementation of the present Covenant.

ARTICLE 23

The States Parties to the present Covenant agree that international action for the achievement of the rights recognised in the present Covenant includes such methods as the conclusion of conventions, the adoption of recommendations, the furnishing of technical assistance and the holding of regional meetings and technical meetings for the purpose of consultation and study organised in conjunction with the Governments concerned.

ARTICLE 24

Nothing in the present Covenant shall be interpreted as impairing the provisions of the Charter of the United Nations and of the constitutions of the specialised agencies which define the respective responsibilities of the various organs of the United Nations and of the specialised agencies in regard to the matters dealt with in the present Covenant.

ARTICLE 25

Nothing in the present Covenant shall be interpreted as impairing the inherent right of all peoples to enjoy and utilise fully and freely their natural wealth and resources.

PART V

ARTICLE 26

1. The present Covenant is open for signature by any State Member of the United Nations or member of any of its specialised agencies, by any State Party to the Statute of the International Court of Justice, and by any other State which has been invited by the General Assembly of the United Nations to become a party to the present Covenant.

2. The present Covenant is subject to ratification. Instruments of ratification shall be deposited with the Secretary-General of the United Nations.

3. The present Covenant shall be open to accession by any State referred to in paragraph 1 of this article.

4. Accession shall be effected by the deposit of an instrument of accession with the Secretary-General of the United Nations.

123

5. The Secretary-General of the United Nations shall inform all States which have signed the present Covenant or acceded to it of the deposit of each instrument of ratification or accession.

ARTICLE 27

1. The present Covenant shall enter into force three months after the date of the deposit with the Secretary-General of the United Nations of the thirty-fifth instrument of ratification or instrument of accession.

2. For each State ratifying the present Covenant or acceding to it after the deposit of the thirty-fifth instrument of ratification or instrument of accession, the present Covenant shall enter into force three months after the date of the deposit of its own instrument of ratification or instrument of accession.

ARTICLE 28

The provisions of the present Covenant shall extend to all parts of federal States without any limitations or exceptions.

ARTICLE 29

1. Any State Party to the present Covenant may propose an amendment and file it with the Secretary-General of the United Nations. The Secretary-General shall thereupon communicate any proposed amendments to the States Parties to the present Covenant with a request that they notify him whether they favour a conference of States Parties for the purpose of considering and voting upon the proposals. In the event that at least one-third of the States Parties favours such a conference, the Secretary-General shall convene the conference under the auspices of the United Nations. Any amendment adopted by a majority of the States Parties present and voting at the conference shall be submitted to the General Assembly of the United Nations for approval.

2. Amendments shall come into force when they have been approved by the General Assembly of the United Nations and accepted by a two-thirds majority of the States Parties to the present Covenant in accordance with their respective constitutional processes.

3. When amendments come into force they shall be binding on those States Parties which have accepted them, other States Parties still being bound by the provisions of the present Covenant and any earlier amendment which they have accepted.

ARTICLE 30

Irrespective of the notifications made under article 26, paragraph 5, the Secretary-General of the United Nations shall inform all States referred to in paragraph 1 of the same article of the following particulars:

(a) Signatures, ratifications and accessions under article 26;
(b) The date of the entry into force of the present Covenant under article 27 and the date of the entry into force of any amendments under article 29.

APPENDIX 5

ARTICLE 31

1. The present Covenant, of which the Chinese, English, French, Russian and Spanish texts are equally authentic, shall be deposited in the archives of the United Nations.

2. The Secretary-General of the United Nations shall transmit certified copies of the present Covenant to all States referred to in article 26.

Appendix 6

prepared by E. D. Brown

STATUS OF MULTILATERAL CONVENTIONS DISCUSSED

(EXCEPT THE COVENANT OF THE LEAGUE OF NATIONS AND THE CHARTER OF THE UNITED NATIONS)

The Conventions concerned have been grouped as follows:

(a) Conventions on Immoral Traffic
(b) Conventions on Slavery and Forced Labour
(c) Conventions on Dangerous Drugs
(d) Conventions on Traffic in Arms
(e) International Covenant on Economic, Social and Cultural Rights
(f) Convention on Suppression of Counterfeiting Currency
(g) Conventions on the Law of the Sea
(h) The Antarctic Treaty
(i) Conventions on Diplomatic and Consular Relations
(j) Conventions on Nuclear Energy
(k) Outer Space Treaty

(a) CONVENTIONS ON IMMORAL TRAFFIC
(STATUS AS AT 1 JANUARY 1970)

I   Convention for the Suppression of the Traffic in Women and Children, 30 September 1921, as amended by Protocol dated 12 November 1947.

II   Convention for the Suppression of the Circulation of, and Traffic in, Obscene Publications, 12 September 1923, as amended by Protocol dated 12 November 1947.

III   Convention for the Suppression of the Traffic in Women of Full Age, 11 October 1933.

IV   Amending Protocol to III above, dated 12 November 1947.

V   Convention for the Suppression of the Traffic in Persons and of the Exploitation of the Prostitution of Others, 21 March 1950.

VI   Final Protocol to IV above, dated 21 March 1950.

Notes

1. Where ratifications, accessions or notifications of succession have been made subject to reservations or declarations, an asterisk (*) is inserted in the table.

2. Two asterisks (**) indicate that the Convention has been denounced.

Dates of ratification, accession, or notification of succession

	I	II	III	IV	V	VI
Afghanistan	12.11.47	12.11.47	10.4.35	12.11.47		
Albania	25.7.49	25.7.49			6.11.58*	6.11.58
Algeria	31.10.63			31.10.63	31.10.63*	
Argentina					15.11.57	1.12.60
Australia	13.11.47	13.11.47	2.9.36	13.11.47		
Austria	7.6.50	4.8.50	7.8.36	7.6.50		
Belgium	12.11.47	12.11.47	11.6.36*	12.11.47	22.6.65	22.6.65
Brazil	6.4.50	3.4.50	24.6.38	6.4.50	12.9.58	12.9.58
Bulgaria			19.12.34		18.1.55*	18.1.55
Burma	13.5.49	13.5.49				
Byelorussian SSR			21.5.48		24.8.56*	24.8.56
Cambodia		30.3.59				
Cameroon			27.10.61			
Canada	24.11.47	24.11.47				
Central African Republic			4.8.62			
Ceylon		15.4.58			15.4.58	7.8.58
Chile			20.3.35			
China	12.11.47	12.11.47				
Congo (Brazzaville)			15.10.62			
Congo (Kinshasa)		31.5.62				
Cuba			25.6.36		4.9.52	4.9.52
Cyprus		16.5.63				
Czechoslovakia	12.11.47	12.11.47	27.7.35	12.11.47	14.3.58	14.3.58
Dahomey			4.4.62			
Denmark	21.11.49	**				
Finland	6.1.49	6.1.49	21.12.36	6.1.49		
France			8.1.47		19.11.60*	
Ghana		7.4.58				
Greece	5.4.60	5.4.60	20.8.37	5.4.60		
Guinea					26.4.62	26.4.62
Guatemala		26.8.49				
Haiti		26.8.53			26.8.53	26.8.53
Hungary	2.2.50	2.2.50	12.8.35	2.2.50	29.9.55*	
India	12.11.47	12.11.47			9.1.53	9.1.53
Iran			12.4.35			
Iraq					22.9.55	
Ireland	19.7.61	28.2.52	25.5.38	19.7.61		
Israel					28.12.50	28.12.50
Italy	5.1.49	16.6.49				
Ivory Coast			8.12.61	5.11.62		
Japan					1.5.58	1.5.58
Jamaica	16.3.65	30.7.64				
Jordan		11.5.59				
Korea (Republic of)					13.2.62	13.2.62
Kuwait					20.11.68	20.11.68
Latvia			17.9.35			
Lebanon	12.11.47					

	I	II	III	IV	V	VI
Libya	17.2.59			17.2.59	3.12.56	3.12.56
Luxembourg	14.3.55	14.3.55		14.3.55		
Madagascar	18.2.63	10.4.63		12.2.64		
Malawi	25.2.66	22.7.65			13.10.65*	
Mali					23.12.64	
Malaysia		21.8.58				
Malta		24.3.67				
Mauritius		18.7.69				
Mexico	12.11.47	4.2.58	3.5.38	12.11.47	21.2.56	21.2.56
Netherlands	7.3.49	7.3.49	20.9.35	7.3.49		
New Zealand		28.10.48				
Nicaragua	24.4.50		12.12.35	24.4.50		
Niger			25.8.61	7.12.64		
Nigeria		26.6.61				
Norway	28.11.47	28.11.47	26.6.35	28.11.47	23.1.52	23.1.52
Pakistan	12.11.47	12.11.47			11.7.52	
Philippines	30.9.54			30.9.54	19.9.52	19.9.52
Poland	21.12.50	21.12.50	8.12.37	21.12.50	2.6.52	2.6.52
Portugal			7.1.37			
Romania	2.11.50	2.11.50	6.6.35	2.11.50	15.2.55*	15.2.55
Senegal			2.5.63			
Sierra Leone	13.8.62	13.3.62				
Singapore	26.10.66			26.10.66	26.10.66	
South Africa	12.11.47	12.11.47	20.11.35	12.11.47	10.10.51	10.10.51
Soviet Union	18.12.47	18.12.47	18.12.47	18.12.47	11.8.54*	11.8.54
Spain					18.6.62	18.6.62
Sudan			13.6.34			
Sweden	9.6.48		25.6.34	9.6.48		
Switzerland			17.7.34			
Syria	17.11.47				12.6.59	12.6.59
Trinidad and Tobago		11.4.66				
Turkey	12.11.47	12.11.47	19.3.41	12.11.47		
Ukrainian SSR					15.11.54*	15.11.54
United Arab Republic	12.11.47	12.11.47			12.6.59	12.6.59
United Kingdom		16.5.49				
United Republic of Tanzania		28.11.62				
Upper Volta					27.8.62	
Venezuela					18.12.68	18.12.68
Yugoslavia	12.11.47	12.11.47			26.4.51	26.4.51

(b) CONVENTIONS ON SLAVERY AND FORCED LABOUR
(STATUS AS AT 1 JANUARY 1970)

I Slavery Convention, 25 September 1926, as amended by Protocol dated 7 December 1953.

II ILO Convention No. 29 concerning Forced or Compulsory Labour, 1930.

III Supplementary Convention on the Abolition of Slavery, the Slave Trade, and Institutions and Practices similar to Slavery, 7 September 1956.

IV ILO Convention No. 105 on the Abolition of Forced Labour, 1957.

Dates of ratification, accession or notification of succession

	I	II	III	IV
Afghanistan	16.8.54		16.11.66	16.5.63
Albania	2.7.57	25.6.57	6.11.58	
Algeria	20.11.63	19.10.62	31.10.63	12.6.69
Argentina		14.3.50	13.8.64	18.1.60
Australia	9.12.53	2.1.32	6.1.58	7.6.60
Austria	16.7.54	7.6.60	7.10.63	5.3.58
Barbados		8.5.67		8.5.67
Belgium	13.12.62	20.1.44	13.12.62	23.1.61
Brazil	6.1.66	25.4.57	6.1.66	18.6.65
Bulgaria		22.9.32	21.8.58	
Burma	29.4.57	4.3.55		
Burundi		11.3.63		11.3.63
Byelorussia	13.9.56	21.8.56	5.6.57	
Cambodia		24.2.69	12.6.57	
Cameroon Eastern		7.6.60		
Cameroon Western		3.9.62		3.9.62
Canada	17.12.53		10.1.63	14.7.59
Central African Republic		27.10.60		9.6.64
Ceylon	21.3.58	5.4.50	21.3.58	
Chad		10.11.60		8.6.61
Chile		31.5.33		
China	14.12.55		28.5.59	31.3.59
Colombia		4.3.69		7.6.63
Congo (Brazzaville)		10.11.60		
Congo (Kinshasa)		20.9.60		
Costa Rica		2.6.60		4.5.59
Cuba	28.6.54	20.7.53	21.8.63	2.6.58
Cyprus		23.9.60	11.5.62	23.9.60
Czechoslovakia		30.10.57	13.6.58	
Dahomey		12.12.60		22.5.61
Denmark	3.3.54	11.2.32	24.4.58	17.1.58
Dominican Republic		5.12.56	31.10.62	23.6.58
Ecuador	17.8.55	6.7.54	29.3.60	5.2.62
El Salvador				18.11.58
Ethiopia	21.1.69		21.1.69	
Finland	19.3.54	13.1.36	1.4.59	27.5.60
France	14.2.63	24.6.37	26.5.64	
Gabon		14.10.60		29.5.61
Germany (Federal Republic)		13.6.56	14.1.59	22.6.59

	I	II	III	IV
Ghana		20.5.57	3.5.63	15.12.58
Greece	12.12.55	13.6.52		30.3.62
Guatemala				9.12.59
Guinea	12.7.62	21.1.59		11.7.61
Guyana		8.6.66		8.6.66
Haiti		4.3.58	12.2.58	4.3.58
Honduras		21.2.57		4.8.58
Hungary	26.2.58	8.6.56	26.2.58	
Iceland		17.2.58	17.11.65	29.11.60
India	12.3.54	30.11.54	23.6.60	
Indonesia		12.6.50		
Iran		10.6.57	30.12.59	13.4.59
Iraq	23.5.55	27.11.62	30.9.63	15.6.59
Ireland	31.8.61	2.3.31	18.9.61	11.6.58
Israel	12.9.55	7.6.55	23.10.57	10.4.58
Italy	4.2.54	18.6.34	12.2.58	15.3.68
Ivory Coast		21.11.60		5.5.61
Jamaica	30.7.64	26.12.62	30.7.64	26.12.62
Japan		21.11.32		
Jordan	5.5.59	6.6.66	27.9.57	31.3.58
Kenya		13.1.64		13.1.64
Kuwait	28.5.63	23.9.68	18.1.63	21.9.61
Laos		23.1.64	9.9.57	
Lesotho		31.10.66		
Liberia	7.12.53	1.5.31		25.5.62
Libya	14.2.57	13.6.61		13.6.61
Luxembourg		24.7.64	1.5.67	24.7.64
Madagascar (Malagasy Republic)	12.2.64	1.11.60		
Malawi	2.8.65		2.8.65	
Malaysia				
States of Malaya		11.11.57	18.11.57	13.10.58
Sabah, Sarawak		3.3.64		3.3.64
Mali		22.9.60		28.5.62
Malta	3.1.66	4.1.65	3.1.66	4.1.65
Mauritania		20.6.61		
Mauritius	18.7.69	2.12.69	18.7.69	2.12.69
Mexico	3.2.54	12.5.34	30.6.59	1.6.59
Monaco	12.11.54			
Mongolia	20.12.68		20.12.68	
Morocco	11.5.59	20.5.57	11.5.59	1.12.66
Nepal	7.1.63		7.1.63	
Netherlands	7.7.55	31.3.53	3.12.57	18.2.59
New Zealand	16.12.53	29.3.38	26.4.62	14.6.68
Nicaragua		12.4.34		31.10.67
Niger	7.12.64	27.2.61	22.7.63	23.3.62
Nigeria	26.6.61	17.10.60	26.6.61	17.10.60
Norway	11.4.57	1.7.32	3.5.60	14.4.58

	I	II	III	IV
Pakistan	30.9.55	23.12.57	20.3.58	15.2.60
Panama		16.5.66		16.5.66
Paraguay		28.8.67		16.5.68
Peru		1.2.60		6.12.60
Philippines	12.7.55		17.11.64	17.11.60
Poland		30.7.58	10.1.63	30.7.58
Portugal		26.6.56	10.8.59	23.11.59
Romania	13.11.57	28.5.57	13.11.57	
Rwanda				18.9.62
San Marino			29.6.67	
Senegal		4.11.60		28.7.61
Sierra Leone	13.3.62	13.6.61	13.3.62	13.6.61
Singapore		25.10.65		25.10.65
Somali Republic		18.11.60		
Ex-British Somaliland				18.11.60
Ex-Trust Territory				8.12.61
South Africa	29.12.53			
Southern Yemen				
(Aden)		14.4.69		14.4.69
Soviet Union	8.8.56	23.6.56	12.4.57	
Spain		29.8.32	21.11.67	6.11.67
Sudan	9.12.57	18.6.57	9.9.57	
Sweden	17.8.54	22.12.31	28.10.59	2.6.58
Switzerland	7.12.53	23.5.40	28.7.64	18.7.58
Syria	4.8.54	26.7.60	17.4.58	23.10.58
Tanzania	28.11.62	Tanganyika 30.1.62	28.11.62	Tanganyika 30.1.62
		Zanzibar 22.6.64		Zanzibar 22.6.64
Thailand		26.2.69		2.12.69
Togo		7.6.60		
Trinidad and Tobago	11.4.66	24.5.63	11.4.66	24.5.63
Tunisia	15.7.66	17.12.62	15.7.66	12.1.59
Turkey	14.1.55		17.7.64	29.3.61
Uganda	12.8.64	4.6.63	12.8.64	4.6.63
Ukraine	27.1.59	10.8.56	3.12.58	
United Arab Republic	29.9.54	29.11.55	17.4.58	23.10.58
United Kingdom	7.12.53	3.6.31	30.4.57	30.12.57
United States of				
America	7.3.56		6.12.67	
Upper Volta		21.11.60		
Uruguay				22.11.68
Venezuela		20.11.44		16.11.64
Vietnam (Republic of)	14.8.56	6.6.53		
Yugoslavia	21.3.55	4.3.33	20.5.58	
Zambia		2.12.64		22.2.65

131

(c) CONVENTIONS ON DANGEROUS DRUGS
(STATUS AS AT 1 JANUARY 1970)

I International Opium Convention, 23 January 1912.
II Convention for the Suppression of the Illicit Traffic in Dangerous Drugs, 26 June 1936, as amended by Protocol dated 11 December 1946.
III Single Convention on Narcotic Drugs, 30 March 1961.

Notes

1. Where ratifications, accessions or notifications of succession have been made subject to reservations or declarations, an asterisk (*) is inserted in the table.
2. Two asterisks (**) indicate that the Convention has been denounced.

Dates of ratification, accession or notification of succession

	I	II	III
Afghanistan	5.5.44		19.3.63
Albania	3.2.25		
Algeria			7.4.65*
Argentina	23.4.46		10.10.63*
Australia			1.12.67*
Austria	16.7.20	17.5.50	
Belgium	16.6.14*	11.12.46	17.10.69
Bolivia	10.1.20		
Brazil	23.12.14	17.12.46	18.6.64
Bulgaria	9.8.20		25.10.68*
Burma			29.7.63*
Byelorussia			20.2.64*
Cambodia	3.10.51	3.10.51	
Cameroon	20.11.61	15.1.62	15.1.62
Canada		11.12.46	11.10.61
Central African Republic	4.9.62		
Ceylon	4.12.57	4.12.57	11.7.63*
Chad			29.1.63
Chile	16.1.23		7.2.68
China	9.2.14	11.12.46	12.5.69
Colombia	26.6.24*	11.12.46	
Congo (Brazzaville)	15.10.62		
Congo (Kinshasa)	31.5.62		
Costa Rica	1.8.24		
Cuba	8.3.20	9.8.67*	30.8.62
Cyprus	16.5.63		30.1.69
Czechoslovakia	10.1.20		20.3.64*
Dahomey			27.4.62
Denmark	10.7.13		15.9.64
Dominican Republic	7.6.23	9.6.58	

	I	II	III
Ecuador	25.2.15		14.1.64
Egypt (and United Arab Republic)	5.6.42	13.9.48	20.7.66*
Estonia	20.4.23		
Ethiopia	28.12.48	9.9.47	29.4.65
Finland	16.5.22		6.7.65
France	10.1.20*	10.10.47	19.2.69*
Gabon			29.2.68
Germany	10.1.20		
Ghana	3.4.58		15.1.64
Great Britain (and United Kingdom)	15.7.14*		2.9.64*
Greece	30.3.20	21.2.49	
Guatemala	27.8.13		1.12.67
Guinea			7.10.68
Haiti	30.6.20	31.5.51	
Honduras	29.8.13		
Hungary	26.7.21		24.4.64*
India		11.12.46	13.12.64*
Indonesia	28.5.58	3.4.58	
Iraq			29.8.62
Israel	12.5.52	16.5.52	23.11.62
Italy	28.6.14	3.4.61*	
Ivory Coast	8.12.61	20.12.61	10.7.62
Jamaica	26.12.63		29.4.64
Japan	10.1.20	7.9.55	13.7.64
Jordan	12.5.58	7.5.58	15.11.62
Kenya			13.11.64
Korea (Republic of)			13.2.62
Kuwait			16.4.62
Laos	7.10.50	13.7.51	
Latvia	25.3.24		
Lebanon	24.5.54		23.4.65
Liberia	30.6.20		
Liechtenstein		24.5.61	
Luxembourg	21.8.22	28.6.55	
Malawi	22.7.65	8.6.65	8.6.65
Malaysia	21.8.58		11.7.67
Mali			15.12.64
Malta	3.1.66		
Mauritius	18.7.69		18.7.69
Mexico	2.4.25	6.5.55*	18.4.67
Monaco	20.2.25		14.8.69
Morocco			4.12.61
Netherlands	28.7.14	**	16.7.65*
New Zealand			26.3.63*
Nicaragua	10.11.14		
Niger	25.8.61		18.4.63

	I	II	III
Nigeria	26.6.61		6.6.69
Norway	12.11.14		1.9.67
Pakistan			9.7.65*
Panama	25.11.20		4.12.63
Paraguay	17.3.43		
Peru	10.1.20		22.7.64
Philippines	30.9.59		2.10.67
Poland	10.1.20		16.3.66*
Portugal	15.12.13		
Romania	14.9.20	11.10.61	
Rwanda	5.5.64		
Salvador	19.9.22		
Saudi Arabia	19.2.43		
Senegal	2.5.63		24.1.64
Sierra Leone	13.3.62		
Soviet Union			20.2.64*
Spain	25.1.19		1.3.66
Sweden	17.4.14*		18.12.64
Switzerland	15.1.25*	31.12.52	
Syria	20.1.54		22.8.62
Thailand	10.7.13*		31.10.61
Togo			6.5.63
Trinidad and Tobago	11.4.66		22.6.64
Tunisia			8.9.64
Turkey	15.9.33	11.12.46	23.5.67
Ukraine			15.4.64*
United States of America	15.12.13		25.5.67*
Upper Volta			16.9.69
Uruguay	3.4.16		
Venezuela	28.10.13		14.2.69
Vietnam (Republic of)	11.8.50		
Yugoslavia			27.8.63
Zambia	10.2.20		12.8.65

(*d*) CONVENTIONS ON TRAFFIC IN ARMS
(STATUS AS AT 1 JANUARY 1970)

I St Germain Convention for the Control of Trade in Arms and Ammunition and Protocol, 10 September 1919. The Convention is not in force.

II International Convention for the Supervision of the International Trade in Arms and Ammunition, with Declaration regarding the Territory of Ifni, 17 June 1925. The Convention is not in force.

III Treaty Regulating the Importation into Ethiopia of Arms, Ammunition and Implements of War, with Declarations and Protocol, 21 August 1930.

Note

The double asterisk (**) following the dates of ratification of Treaty III by France and the United Kingdom, indicates that the Italian Government was notified on 19 October 1938 that the Governments of France and the United Kingdom regarded the Treaty as no longer operative.

Dates of ratification or accession

	I	II	III
Brazil	22.12.19		
Bulgaria	13.9.21		
Chile	5.8.20		
China	2.10.20		
Estonia	17.10.23		
Ethiopia	27.9.23		19.2.32
Finland	31.6.21		
France			19.2.32**
Greece	24.8.20		
Guatemala	22.1.20		
Haiti	3.3.20		
Iran	27.3.20		
Italy			19.2.32
Muscat	9.6.21		
Peru	31.1.20		
Portugal	17.7.22		
Romania	31.5.24		
Thailand	30.3.21		
United Kingdom		British Empire 6.2.30	19.2.32**
Uruguay	5.2.25		
Venezuela	8.3.20		

(*e*) INTERNATIONAL COVENANT ON ECONOMIC, SOCIAL AND CULTURAL RIGHTS, 19 DECEMBER 1966 (STATUS AS AT 1 JANUARY 1970)

Dates of ratification or accession

Colombia	29.10.69
Costa Rica	29.11.68
Cyprus	2.4.69
Ecuador	6.3.69
Syria	21.4.69*
Tunisia	18.3.69

* Subject to a reservation.

(*f*) CONVENTION ON SUPPRESSION OF COUNTERFEITING CURRENCY (STATUS AS AT 1 JANUARY 1970)

I Convention for the Suppression of Counterfeiting Currency, 20 April 1929.
II Protocol of same date.

135

Note

Ratifications or accessions made subject to reservations or declarations are marked by an asterisk (*).

Dates of ratification, accession or notification of succession

	I	II
Algeria	17.3.65*	17.3.65
Austria	25.6.31	25.6.31
Belgium	6.6.32	
Brazil	1.7.38	1.7.38
Bulgaria	22.5.30	22.5.30
Ceylon	2.6.67	2.6.67
Colombia	9.5.32	9.5.32
Cuba	13.6.33	13.6.33
Cyprus	10.6.65	10.6.65
Czechoslovakia	12.9.31	12.9.31
Dahomey	17.3.66	
Denmark	19.2.31*	
Ecuador	25.9.37	
Estonia	30.8.30	30.8.30
Finland	25.9.36	25.9.36
France	28.3.58	
Gabon	11.8.64	11.8.64
Germany	3.10.33	
Ghana	9.7.64	9.7.64
Greece	19.5.31	19.5.31
Holy See	1.3.65	
Hungary	14.6.33	
Iraq	14.5.65	14.5.65
Ireland	24.7.34	
Israel	10.2.65	10.2.65
Italy	27.12.35	
Ivory Coast	25.5.64	25.5.64
Kuwait	9.12.68	
Latvia	22.7.39	22.7.39
Lebanon	6.10.66	
Malawi	18.11.65	18.11.65
Mauritius	18.7.69	18.7.69
Mexico	30.3.36	
Monaco	21.10.31	
Netherlands	30.4.32	
Niger	5.5.69	5.5.69
Norway	16.3.31*	
Poland	15.6.34	15.6.34
Portugal	18.9.30	18.9.30
Romania	7.3.39	10.11.30
San Marino	18.10.67	

	I	II
Senegal	25.8.65	25.8.65
South Africa	29.8.67	
Soviet Union	13.7.31	
Spain	28.4.30	28.4.30
Switzerland	30.12.58	
Syria	14.8.64	
Thailand	6.6.63	
Turkey	21.1.37	
Uganda	15.4.65	
United Arab Republic	15.7.57	
United Kingdom	28.7.59	
Upper Volta	8.12.64	8.12.64
Vietnam (Republic of)	3.12.64	3.12.64
Yugoslavia	24.11.30	24.11.30

(g) CONVENTIONS ON THE LAW OF THE SEA
(STATUS AS AT 1 JANUARY 1970)

I   Barcelona Convention and Statute on Freedom of Transit, 20 April 1921.

II   International Convention for the Prevention of Pollution of the Sea by Oil, 12 May 1954, as amended 13 April 1962 (The further amendments approved by the IMCO Assembly in October 1969 had received no acceptances by 1 January 1970).

III   Geneva Convention on the Territorial Sea and the Contiguous Zone, 29 April 1958.

IV   Geneva Convention on the High Seas, 29 April 1958.

V   Geneva Convention on Fishing and Conservation of the Living Resources of the High Seas, 29 April 1958.

VI   Geneva Convention on the Continental Shelf, 29 April 1958.

VII   Optional Protocol of Signature concerning the Compulsory Settlement of Disputes, 29 April 1958.

VIII   International Convention for the Safety of Life at Sea, 17 June 1960 (Amendments adopted by IMCO Assembly on 30 November 1966, 25 October 1967 and 26 November 1968 are not yet in force).

IX   International Regulations for Preventing Collisions at Sea, 1960, 17 June 1960.

X   Convention on Transit Trade of Land-locked States, 8 July 1965.

Notes

1. Where ratifications, accessions or notifications of succession have been made subject to reservations or declarations, an asterisk (*) is inserted in the table.

2. The letter 'A' indicates that a State has agreed to accept and apply the International Regulations for Preventing Collisions at Sea, 1960. The Regulations became applicable by accepting Governments on 1 September 1965.

137

Dates of ratification, accession or notification of succession

	I	II	III	IV	V	VI	VII	VIII	IX	X
Afghanistan										
Albania	8.10.21			28.4.59						
Algeria		20.1.64		7.12.64*		7.12.64				
Argentina								20.1.64*	A	
Australia								27.4.66	A	
Austria	15.11.23	29.8.62	14.5.63	14.5.63	14.5.63	14.5.63		20.12.67		
Belgium	16.5.27	16.4.57						10.1.66	A	
Brazil								8.3.67	A	
Bulgaria	11.7.22		31.8.62*	31.8.62*		31.8.62		16.10.67	A	
Burma								12.7.65	A	
Burundi										1.5.68
Byelorussia			27.2.61*	27.2.61*		27.2.61				
Cambodia			18.3.60	18.3.60	18.3.60	18.3.60				
Cameroon									A	
Canada		19.12.56						26.5.65	A	
Central African Republic				15.10.62						
Chad										
Chile	19.3.28							7.9.66		2.3.67
China								23.2.65	A	
Colombia					3.1.63	8.1.62				
Congo (Democratic Republic of)								20.5.68		
Cuba								22.8.63		
Cyprus								27.7.65	A	
Czechoslovakia	29.10.23		31.8.61*	31.8.61*		31.8.61		5.7.67	A	8.8.67*

138

	I	II	III	IV	V	VI	VII	VIII	IX	X
Denmark	13.11.22	26.11.56	26.9.68	26.9.68	26.9.68*	12.6.63	26.9.68	1.12.64	A	26.3.69
Dominican Republic		29.5.63	11.8.64	11.8.64	11.8.64	11.8.64				
Estonia	6.6.25									
Ethiopia					16.2.65					
Finland	29.1.23	30.12.58	16.2.65			16.2.65	16.2.65	11.5.65	A	
France	19.9.24	26.7.57				14.6.65*		16.10.61	A	
Gambia								1.11.66	A	
Germany (Federal Republic)	9.4.24	11.6.56						26.5.65*	A	
Ghana		17.5.62						22.3.62	A	
Greece	18.2.24	28.3.67						13.2.63	A	
Guatemala				27.11.61		27.11.61				
Guinea								5.9.68		
Haiti			29.3.60	29.3.60	29.3.60	29.3.60	29.3.60	17.3.61		
Honduras								18.2.69		18.9.67*
Hungary	18.5.28		6.12.61*	6.12.61*						
Iceland		23.2.62						11.12.64	A	
India	2.8.22							28.2.66	A	
Indonesia				10.8.61*				26.10.66	A	
Iran	29.1.31							31.5.66		
Iraq	1.3.30									
Ireland		13.2.57						14.2.67	A	
Israel		11.11.65	6.9.61	6.9.61		6.9.61		5.10.65	A	
Italy	5.8.22	25.5.64*	17.12.64*	17.12.64				26.5.66	A	
Ivory Coast		17.3.67						2.11.65	A	
Jamaica			8.10.65	8.10.65	16.4.64	8.10.65		22.2.68	A	
Japan	20.2.24	21.8.67	10.6.68	10.6.68				23.4.63	A	

139

	I	II	III	IV	V	VI	VII	VIII	IX	X
Jordan		8.5.63								
Kenya								21.5.65	A	
Korea (Republic of)			20.6.69	20.6.69	20.6.69	20.6.69		14.5.65*	A	29.12.67
Kuwait		27.11.61								
Laos	24.11.56									
Latvia	29.9.23									
Lebanon		31.5.67						27.4.66	A	
Lesotho										
Liberia		28.3.62*						26.5.64	A	28.5.69
Luxembourg	19.3.30									
Madagascar (Malagasy Republic)		1.2.65								
Malawi			31.7.62	31.7.62	31.7.62	31.7.62		13.9.62	A	12.12.66
Malaysia			3.11.65	3.11.65	3.11.65	3.11.65		16.8.65	A	
Maldives			21.12.60	21.12.60	21.12.60	21.12.60		29.1.68	A	11.10.67
Mali										
Malta	13.5.66		19.5.66		19.5.66	19.5.66	19.5.66			
Mauritania	18.7.69							4.12.67		
Mauritius										
Mexico		10.5.56	2.8.66*	2.8.66*	2.8.66	2.8.66		22.6.66	A	
Mongolia										
Morocco		29.2.68						28.11.62		26.7.66*
Nauru								19.1.70		
Nepal	22.8.66			28.12.62				16.10.64		
Netherlands	17.4.24	24.7.58	18.2.66	18.2.66	18.2.66	18.2.66	18.2.66	14.1.66	A	22.8.66
New Zealand	2.8.22					18.1.65			A	

	I	II	III	IV	V	VI	VII	VIII	IX	X
Nicaragua								9.10.67		
Niger	3.11.67	22.1.68							A	3.6.66
Nigeria	4.9.23	26.1.57	26.6.61	26.6.61	26.6.61			30.11.65	A	16.5.66
Norway								23.8.61	A	17.9.68
Pakistan								24.2.66*	A	
Panama		25.9.63						12.10.65		
Paraguay								11.9.63	A	
Peru								25.7.62	A	
Philippines	8.10.24	19.11.63						11.8.65	A	
Poland		28.2.61*		29.6.62*	29.6.62	29.6.62		29.4.66	A	
Portugal		28.3.67*	8.1.63	8.1.63	8.1.63	8.1.63	8.1.63	14.6.66	A	
Romania	5.9.23		12.12.61*	12.12.61*		12.12.61		12.12.66*	A	
Rwanda	10.2.65									13.8.68
San Marino										12.6.68
Saudi Arabia								3.5.65	A	
Senegal			25.4.61	25.4.61	25.4.61	25.4.61				
Sierra Leone			13.3.62	13.3.62	13.3.62	25.11.66				
Singapore								12.2.69	A	
Somalia								30.3.67		
South Africa			9.4.63	9.4.63	9.4.63	9.4.63		13.12.67	A	
Southern Yemen		20.5.69						20.5.69		
Soviet Union		3.9.69	22.11.60*	22.11.60*		22.11.60		4.8.65		
Spain	17.12.29	20.1.64						22.1.63	A	
Swaziland	24.11.69									26.5.6⊡
Sweden	19.1.25	24.5.56				1.6.66	28.6.66	23.12.65	A	
Switzerland	14.7.24	12.1.66	18.5.66	18.5.66	18.5.66	18.5.66	18.5.66	12.1.66	A	
Syria		24.12.68						24.12.68		

	I	II	III	IV	V	VI	VII	VIII	IX	X
Thailand	29.11.22									
Trinidad and Tobago			2.7.68	2.7.68	2.7.68	2.7.68		6.9.66	A	
Tunisia			11.4.66	11.4.66	11.4.66	11.7.68		20.5.63		
Turkey	27.6.33							2.6.66	A	25.3.69
Uganda			14.9.64	14.9.64	14.9.64	14.9.64				
Ukraine			12.1.61*	12.1.61*		12.1.61				
United Arab Republic		22.4.63						27.7.65*	A	
United Kingdom	2.8.22*	6.5.55	14.3.60*	14.3.60*	14.3.60*	11.5.64		11.6.64*	A	
United States of America		8.9.61*	12.4.61	12.4.61	12.4.61*	12.4.61		2.8.62	A	29.10.68
				4.10.65	4.10.65					
Upper Volta								19.9.68		
Uruguay		12.12.63	15.8.61*	15.8.61	10.7.63	15.8.61*		23.1.69		
Venezuela								8.1.62	A	
Vietnam (Republic of)							28.1.66	23.2.65	A	
Yugoslavia	7.5.30		28.1.66	28.1.66	28.1.66	28.1.66*				10.5.67
Zambia										2.12.66

142

(h) THE ANTARCTIC TREATY
(STATUS AS AT 1 JANUARY 1970)

I   The Antarctic Treaty, 1 December 1959.

Date of ratification or accession

Argentina	23.6.61
Australia	23.6.61
Belgium	26.7.60
Chile	23.6.61
Czechoslovakia	14.6.62
Denmark	20.5.65
France	16.9.60
Japan	4.8.60
Netherlands	30.3.67
New Zealand	1.11.60
Norway	24.8.60
Poland	8.6.61
South Africa	21.6.60
Soviet Union	2.11.60
United Kingdom	31.5.60
United States	18.8.60

(i) CONVENTIONS ON DIPLOMATIC AND CONSULAR RELATIONS
(STATUS AS AT 1 JANUARY 1970)

I   Vienna Convention on Diplomatic Relations, 18 April 1961.
II   Vienna Convention on Consular Relations, 24 April 1963.

Note

Where ratifications, accessions or notifications of succession have been made subject to reservations or declarations, an asterisk (*) is inserted in the table.

Dates of ratification, accession or notification of succession

	I	II
Afghanistan	6.10.65	
Algeria	14.4.64	14.4.64
Argentina	10.10.63	7.3.67
Australia	26.1.68*	
Austria	28.4.66	12.6.69
Barbados	6.5.68	
Belgium	2.5.68*	
Botswana	11.4.69*	
Brazil	25.3.65	11.5.67
Bulgaria	17.1.68*	

143

	I	II
Burundi	1.5.68	
Byelorussia	14.5.64*	
Cambodia	31.8.65*	
Cameroon		22.5.67
Canada	26.5.66*	
Chile	9.1.68	9.1.68
China	19.12.69	
Congo (Brazzaville)	11.3.63	
Congo (Kinshasa)	19.7.65	
Costa Rica	9.11.64	29.12.66
Cuba	26.9.63*	15.10.65*
Cyprus	10.9.68	
Czechoslovakia	24.5.63	13.3.68*
Dahomey	27.3.67	
Denmark	2.10.68*	
Dominican Republic	14.1.64	4.3.64
Ecuador	21.9.64	11.3.65
El Salvador	9.12.65	
Finland	9.12.69	
Gabon	2.4.64	23.2.65
Germany	11.11.64*	
Ghana	28.6.62	4.10.63
Guatemala	1.10.63*	
Guinea	10.1.68	
Holy See	17.4.64	
Honduras	13.2.68	13.2.68
Hungary	24.9.65*	
India	15.10.65	
Iran	3.2.65	
Iraq	15.10.63*	
Ireland	10.5.67	10.5.67
Italy	25.6.69	25.6.69*
Ivory Coast	1.10.62	
Jamaica	5.6.63	
Japan	8.6.64*	
Kenya	1.7.65	1.7.65
Kuwait	23.7.69*	
Laos	3.12.62	
Lesotho	26.11.69	
Liberia	15.5.62	
Liechtenstein	8.5.64	18.5.66
Luxembourg	17.8.66*	
Madagascar	31.7.63	17.2.67
Malawi	19.5.65	
Malaysia	9.11.65	
Mali	28.3.68	28.3.68
Malta	7.3.67*	

144

	I	II
Mauritania	16.7.62	
Mauritius	18.7.69	
Mexico	16.6.65	16.6.65*
Mongolia (People's Republic)	5.1.67*	
Morocco	19.6.68*	
Nepal	28.9.65*	28.9.65
Niger	5.12.62	26.4.66
Nigeria	19.6.67	22.1.68
Norway	24.10.67	
Pakistan	29.3.62	14.4.69
Panama	4.12.63	28.8.67
Paraguay	23.12.69	
Peru	18.12.68	
Philippines	15.11.65	15.11.65
Poland	19.4.65	
Portugal	11.9.68*	
Romania	15.11.68*	
Rwanda	15.4.64	
San Marino	8.9.65	
Senegal		29.4.66
Sierra Leone	13.8.62	
Somalia	29.3.68	29.3.68
Soviet Union	25.3.64*	
Spain	21.11.67	
Swaziland	25.4.69	
Sweden	21.3.67	
Switzerland	30.10.63	3.5.65
Tanzania	5.11.62*	
Trinidad and Tobago	19.10.65	19.10.65
Tunisia	24.1.68	8.7.64
Uganda	15.4.65	
Ukraine	12.6.64*	
United Arab Republic	9.6.64*	21.6.65*
United Kingdom	1.9.64*	
United States of America		24.11.69
Upper Volta		11.8.64
Venezuela	16.3.65*	27.10.65
Yugoslavia	1.4.63	8.2.65

(j) CONVENTIONS ON NUCLEAR ENERGY

I   Treaty Banning Nuclear Weapon Tests in the Atmosphere, in Outer Space and Under Water, 5 August 1963.
(STATUS AS AT 1 JANUARY 1970).

II   Treaty on the Non-proliferation of Nuclear Weapons, 1 July 1968.
(STATUS AS AT 1 APRIL 1970).

Note

Where ratifications, accessions or notifications of succession have been
made subject to a declaration or statement, an asterisk (*) is inserted in the
table.

Dates of ratification, accession or notification of succession

	I	II
Afghanistan	12.3.64	5.3.70
Australia	12.11.63	
Austria	17.7.64	27.6.69
Belgium	1.3.66	
Bolivia	25.1.66	
Botswana	5.1.68	28.4.69
Brazil	4.3.65	
Bulgaria	2.12.63	3.11.69
Burma	15.11.63	
Cameroon		8.1.69
Canada	28.1.64	8.1.69
Central African Republic	24.8.65	
Ceylon	13.2.64	
Chad	1.3.65	
Chile	6.10.65	
China (Taiwan)	18.5.64	27.1.70
Congo (Kinshasa)	28.10.65	
Costa Rica	10.7.67	3.3.70
Cyprus	15.4.65	5.3.70
Czechoslovakia	14.10.63	22.7.69
Dahomey	22.4.65	
Denmark	15.1.64	3.1.69
Dominican Republic	18.6.64	
Ecuador	8.5.64	7.3.69
El Salvador	7.12.64	
Ethiopia		5.3.70
Finland	9.1.64	5.2.69
Gabon	4.3.64	
Gambia	6.5.65	
Germany (Democratic Republic)	30.12.63	31.10.69
Germany (Federal Republic)	1.12.64*	
Ghana	27.11.63	
Greece	18.12.63	
Guatemala	6.1.64*	
Honduras	2.12.64	
Hungary	21.10.63	27.5.69

146

	I	II
Iceland	29.4.64	18.7.69
India	10.10.63	
Indonesia	8.5.64	
Iran	5.5.64	5.3.70
Iraq	30.11.64	29.10.69
Ireland	18.12.63	4.7.68
Israel	15.1.64	
Italy	10.12.64	
Ivory Coast	5.2.65	
Jamaica		5.3.70
Japan	15.6.64	
Jordan	29.5.64	11.2.70
Kenya	10.6.65	
Korea (Republic)	24.7.64*	
Kuwait	21.5.65*	
Laos	10.2.65	5.3.70
Lebanon	20.5.65	
Liberia	22.5.64	5.3.70
Libya	15.7.68	
Luxembourg	10.2.65	
Malagasy Republic	15.3.65	
Malawi	7.1.65	
Malaysia	16.7.64	5.3.70
Mali		5.3.70
Malta	1.12.64	6.2.70
Mauritania	15.4.64	
Mauritius	12.5.69	14.4.69
Mexico	27.12.63	21.1.69*
Mongolia	7.11.63	14.5.69
Morocco	1.2.66	
Nepal	7.10.64	3.2.70
Netherlands	14.9.64	
New Zealand	10.10.63	10.9.69
Nicaragua	26.1.65	
Niger	6.7.64	
Nigeria	17.2.67	27.9.68
Norway	21.11.63	5.2.69
Panama	24.2.66	
Paraguay		5.3.70
Peru	4.8.64	3.3.70
Philippines	10.11.65*	
Poland	14.10.63	12.6.69
Romania	12.12.63	4.2.70
Rwanda	22.10.63	
San Marino	3.7.64	
Senegal	6.5.64	
Sierra Leone	21.2.64	

	I	II
Singapore	23.7.68	
Somali Republic		5.3.70
South Africa	10.10.63	
Soviet Union	10.10.63	5.3.70
Spain	17.12.64	
Sudan	4.3.66	
Swaziland	29.5.69	11.12.69
Sweden	9.12.63	9.1.70
Switzerland	16.1.64	
Syria	1.6.64	24.9.69
Tanzania	6.2.64	
Thailand	15.11.63	
Togo	7.12.64	26.2.70
Trinidad and Tobago	16.7.64	
Tunisia	26.5.65	26.2.70
Turkey	8.7.65	
Uganda	24.3.64	
United Arab Republic	10.1.64*	
United Kingdom	10.10.63	27.11.68*
United States of America	10.10.63	5.3.70
Upper Volta		3.3.70
Uruguay	25.2.69	
Venezuela	3.3.65	
Western Samoa	19.1.65	
Yugoslavia	15.1.64	5.3.70*
Zambia	8.2.65	

(k) OUTER SPACE TREATY
(STATUS AS AT 1 APRIL 1970)

I Treaty Governing the Exploration and Use of Outer Space, including the Moon and Other Celestial Bodies, 27 January 1967.

Note

Where ratifications or accessions have been made subject to a declaration, an asterisk (*) is inserted in the table.

Dates of ratification or accession

Argentina	26.3.69	Canada	10.10.67
Australia	10.10.67	Czechoslovakia	11.5.67
Austria	26.2.68	Denmark	10.10.67
Barbados	12.9.68	Dominican Republic	26.11.68
Brazil	5.3.69	Ecuador	7.3.69
Bulgaria	19.4.67	El Salvador	15.1.69
Burma	18.3.70	Finland	12.7.67

148

Germany, (Democratic		Poland	30.1.68
Republic)	2.2.67	Romania	9.4.68
Hungary	26.6.67	San Marino	3.2.69
Iceland	5.2.68	Sierra Leone	25.10.67
Iraq	23.9.69	South Africa	8.10.68
Ireland	19.7.68	Soviet Union	10.10.67
Japan	10.10.67	Spain	27.11.68
Lebanon	31.3.69	Sweden	11.10.67
Malagasy Republic	22.8.68	Switzerland	18.12.69
Mali	11.6.68	Syria	19.11.68
Mauritius	21.4.69	Thailand	5.9.68
Mexico	31.1.68	Tunisia	28.3.68
Mongolia	10.10.67	Turkey	27.3.68
Morocco	21.12.67	Uganda	24.4.68
Nepal	10.10.67	United Arab Republic	10.10.67
Netherlands	10.10.69	United Kingdom	10.10.67*
New Zealand	31.5.68	United States of	
Niger	17.4.67	America	10.10.67
Nigeria	14.11.67	Upper Volta	18.6.68
Norway	1.7.69	Uruguay	18.6.68
Pakistan	8.4.68	Venezuela	3.3.70

149

FURTHER READING

CHAPTERS I–III

Broms, B., *Finland and the League of Nations*, 1963.
Brownlie, I., *Principles of Public International Law*, 1966 (Ch. XI).
Bülck, H., 'Frauenhandel' in H.-J. Schlochauer (ed.), *Wörterbuch des Voelkerrechts*, Vol. I (1960).
Carlston, K. S., *Law and Organisation in World Society*, 1962.
—— 'World order and international law', 20 *Journal of Legal Education* (1968).
Carnegie Endowment for International Peace, European Centre, *The Concept of* Jus Cogens *in International Law*, 1967.
Coursier, H., 'The slave question', *Revue internationale de la Croix-Rouge* (1954).
Erler, G., 'Internationales Wirtschaftsrecht' in K. Strupp and H.-J. Schlochauer (eds.), *Wörterbuch des Voelkerrechts*, Vol. III (1962).
Fawcett, J. E. S., 'Trade and finance in international law', Hague Academy of International Law, *Recueil*, Vol. 123 (1968).
Fitzmaurice, E., 'Convention on Counterfeiting Currency', 26 *A.J.I.L.* (1932).
Holthouse, H., *Cannibal Cargoes*, 1969.
Greenidge, C. W. W., *Slavery*, 1958.
Hailey, Lord, *An African Survey*, 1945 (Ch. XI).
Higgins, R., *Conflict of Interests*, 1965 (Ch. 2).
Hill, M., *The Economic and Financial Organisation of the League of Nations*, 1946.
Katz, M., and Brewster, K., *International Transactions and Relations*, 1960 (Ch. 12).
Kemper, M., and Kirsten, J., *Imperialistisches Internationales Wirtschaftsrecht und Souveraenitaet*, 1967.
McNair, Lord, 'The general principles of law recognised by civilised nations', 33 *B.Y.I.L.* (1957).
McDougal, M. S., *et al.*, *Studies in World Public Order*, 1960.
Mann, F. A., 'Reflections on a commercial law of nations', 33 *B.Y.I.L.* (1957).
Metzger, S. D., *Law of International Trade*, 1966 (two vols.).
Mueller, G. O. W., and Wise, E. M. (eds.), *International Criminal Law*, 1965.
Renborg, B. A., *International Drug Control*, 1947.
Royal Institute of International Affairs, *International Sanctions*, 1938.
Schwarzenberger, G., 'The principles and standards of international economic law', Hague Academy of International Law, *Recueil*, Vol. 117 (1966).
—— 'Law, order and legitimation', 23 *Current Legal Problems* (1970).
Schmitthoff, C. M. (ed.), *The Sources of the Law of International Trade*, 1964.

Stankiewicz, W. J. (ed.), *In Defence of Sovereignty*, 1969.
Starke, J. G., *Studies in International Law*, 1965 (Ch. 3).
Terry, C. E., and Pellen, M., *The Opium Problem*, 1928.
United Nations, *The Suppression of Slavery* (1951.XIV.2).
Willis, H. P., *A History of the Latin Monetary Union*, 1901.
Wortley, B. A., 'The interaction of public and private international law', Hague Academy of International Law, *Recueil*, Vol. 85 (1954).
—— *Jurisprudence*, 1967 (Ch. 1).

CHAPTERS IV–V

Alexandrowicz, C. H., *World Economic Agencies*, 1962.
Arzinger, R., *Das Selbstbestimmungsrecht im allgemeinen Völkerrecht der Gegenwart*, 1966.
Asamoah, O. Y., *The Legal Significance of the Declarations of the General Assembly of the United Nations*, 1966.
Banerjee, S. K., 'The concept of permanent sovereignty over natural resources', 8 *Indian J.I.L.* (1968).
Bloomfield, L. P., 'Arms control and international order', 23 *International Organisation* (1969).
Bornecque-Winandy, E., *Droits de l'O.N.U. et stratégies économiques spatiales*, 1969.
Bowett, D. W., *The Law of the Sea*, 1967.
—— *The Law of International Institutions*, 1970 (Part One).
Brehme, G., *Souveraenitaet der jungen Nationalstaaten ueber Naturreichtuemer*, 1967.
Brown, E. D., 'The legal regime of inner space', 22 *Year Book of World Affairs* (1968).
—— 'The legal regime of inner space: military aspects', 22 *Current Legal Problems* (1969).
Buergenthal, T. H., *Law-making in the International Civil Aviation Organisation*, 1969.
Cahier, P., and Lee, L. T., 'Vienna Conventions on Diplomatic and Consular Relations', No. 571 *International Conciliation* (1969).
Cheng, B., 'Le traité de 1967 sur l'espace', 95 *J. Droit international* (1968).
Clark, G., and Sohn, L. B., *World Peace through World Law*, 1960.
Cooper, R., *The Economics of Interdependence: economic policy in the Atlantic community*, 1968.
Cox, R. W. (ed.), 'International organisation: world politics', *Studies in Economic and Social Agencies*, 1969.
Curzon, G., *Multilateral Commercial Diplomacy*, 1965.
Douglas-Home, C., 'The arms sales race', 23 *Year Book of World Affairs* (1969).
Doxey, M. P., *Economic Sanctions in the Enforcement Process*, 1970.
Falk, R. A., 'World population and international law', 63 *A.J.I.L.* (1969).
Fawcett, J. E. S., *International Law and the Uses of Outer Space*, 1968.
Finkelstein, L. S. (ed.), 'The United States and international organisation', 23 *International Organisation* (1969).

Firmage, E. B., 'The Treaty on the Non-Proliferation of Nuclear Weapons', 63 *A.J.I.L.* (1969).
Fried, J. H. E., 'The 1965 Convention on Transit Trade of Land-locked States', 6 *Indian J.I.L.* (1966).
Friedmann, W., *The Changing Structure of International Law*, 1964 (Ch. 17).
Galbraith, J. K., *The New Industrial State*, 1967.
Gardner, R. N., and Millikan, M. F. (eds.), 'The global partnership: international agencies and economic development', 22 *International Organisation* (1968).
Green, L. C., 'Human rights in public international law' in L. M. Singhvi (ed.), *Horizons of Freedom*, 1969.
—— 'Southern Rhodesian independence', 14 *Archiv des Voelkerrechts* (1969).
Gutteridge, J., 'Supplementary Slavery Convention, 1956', 6 *I.C.L.Q.* (1957).
Haas, E. B., *Tangles of Hopes: American commitments and world order*, 1969.
Halderman, J. W., 'Some legal aspects of sanctions in the Rhodesian case', 17 *I.C.L.Q.* (1968).
Hanessian, J., 'The Antarctic Treaty, 1959', 9 *I.C.L.Q.* (1960).
International Labour Office. *Report* of the *ad hoc* Committee on Forced Labour, 1953.
Johnson, D. H. N., 'Sanctions against South Africa: the legal aspect' in R. Segal (ed.), *Sanctions against South Africa*, 1964.
—— *Rights in Air Space*, 1965.
Kirdar, Ü., *The Structure of United Nations Economic Aid to Under-developed Countries*, 1966.
Jenks, C. W., *Human Rights and International Labour Standards*, 1960.
—— *Beyond the Charter*, 1968.
—— *A new world of law?* 1969.
Jessup, P. H., and Taubenfeld, H. J., *Controls for Outer Space and the Antarctic Analogy*, 1959.
Kimminich, O., *Voelkerrecht im Atomzeitalter der Atomsperr vertrag und seine Folgen*, 1969.
Landy, E. A., *The Effectiveness of International Supervision: thirty years of I.L.O. experience*, 1966.
Lauterpacht, H., *International Law and Human Rights*, 1950 (Chs. 9–10).
Leiss, A. C., *Apartheid and United Nations*, 1965.
Macdonald, R. St J., 'The resort to economic coercion by international political organisations', 17 *Univ. Toronto L.J.* (1967).
Magdoff, H., *The Age of Imperialism: the economics of U.S. foreign policy*, 1969.
Meerhaeghe, M. A. G. van, *International Economic Institutions*, 1966.
Minty, A. S., *South Africa's Defence Strategy*, 1969.
Moeller, H., 'Weltwirtschaftsordnung und internationale Wirtschafts-organisation', 3 *Berichte der deutschen Gesellschaft fuer Voelkerrecht* (1959).
Mughraby, M. A., *Permanent Sovereignty over Oil Resources*, 1966.

Muhammad, S., *The Legal Framework of World Trade*, 1958.

Nwogugu, E. I., *Legal Problems of Foreign Investment in Developing Countries*, 1965.

Pépin, E., 'A legal order for outer space' in E. McWhinney and M. A. Balder (eds.), *New Frontiers in Space Law*, 1969.

Rajan, M. S., *United Nations and Domestic Jurisdiction*, 1961.

Roucounas, E. J., 'L'équilibre entre la non-prolifération des armes nucléaires, la prolifération des connaissances nucléaires "civiles" et les garanties de sécurité nucléaire', 21 *Revue Hellénique de Droit International* (1969).

Schwarzenberger, G., *Foreign Investments and International Law*, 1969 (Ch. 12).

Schwelb, E., 'The nuclear test ban treaty and international law', 58 *A.J.I.L.* (1964).

—— 'Civil and political rights: the international measures of implementation', 62 *A.J.I.L.* (1968).

Sharp, W. R., *The United Nations Economic and Social Council*, 1969.

Skubiszewski, K., 'The application of non-military measures by the General Assembly of the United Nations', 1 *Polish Yearbook of International Law* (1966–7).

Strange, S., 'The strategic trade embargoes', 12 *Year Book of World Affairs* (1958).

Thayer, G., *The War Business*, 1969.

Tinbergen, J., *International Economic Integration*, 1965.

Tunkin, G. I., 'The legal nature of the United Nations', Hague Academy of International Law, *Recueil*, Vol. 119 (1966).

—— 'A universal international organisation: illusion and reality', 1 *Eastern Journal of International Law* (1969).

United Nations, *The Status of Permanent Sovereignty over Natural Wealth and Resources*, 1962.

—— *A Study of the Capacity of the United Nations Development System*, 1969 (two vols.).

Unitar (United Nations Institute for Training and Research), *Wider Acceptance of Multilateral Treaties*, 1969.

United States Government Printing Office, *The United Nations Conference on International Organisation. Selected Documents*, 1946.

White, G., *Nationalisation of Foreign Property*, 1961.

Wortley, B. A., *Expropriation in Public International Law*, 1959.

—— 'Les conditions juridiques des investissements de capitaux dans les pays en voie de développement et des accords y relatifs', 52 (I) *Annuaire de l'Institut de Droit International* (1967).

—— 'Some observations on claims for violations by a State of the human rights of a citizen', 7 *Rivista di Diritto Europeo* (1968).

Zacklin, R., 'Challenge of Rhodesia', No. 575 *International Conciliation* (1969).

INDEX